# Disrupt Your Default

## Rethink, Reclaim, Redefine Your Life

### Mea Brown

Shadow Scribe Media

For permissions, inquiries, or licensing requests, please contact: Mea@meabrown.com

Cover Design by Shadow Scribe Media

Book Interior Design by Shadow Scribe Media

www.meabrown.com

**Memoir Disclaimer**

While this book is not a memoir, it does contain the retelling of personal historical events. The events and experiences shared in *Disrupt Your Default* are true to the best of my memory and recollection. They are presented as I experienced and understood them at the time. However, memory is imperfect, and perspectives differ. Not all family members, friends, or individuals mentioned were aware of these events as they unfolded, and their own recollections may vary—especially if their interactions with the people and situations described were different from mine. This book is not intended to cause harm, misrepresent, or disparage anyone. Any resemblance to specific individuals outside of my own lived experience is purely coincidental.

This book is a deeply personal account, and while I have taken care to be truthful, it is ultimately my story as I lived it. Names and certain details may have been changed for privacy and clarity.

**Advice Disclaimer**

The insights and guidance shared in *Disrupt Your Default* are based on my personal experiences and what has worked for me. I am not a licensed therapist, psychologist, or medical professional, and nothing in this book should be taken as medical, psychological, or professional advice. Readers should use their own judgment and seek appropriate professional support when needed.

Any progress, growth, or transformation a reader experiences will depend on their own unique circumstances, efforts, and actions. I cannot guarantee specific outcomes, as every individual's journey is different. This book is meant to inspire and empower, not to serve as a substitute for professional help or guidance.

# Contents

# Dedication

For my unfailingly loving and supportive husband, Steve. My partner, my encourager, my defender, and my best friend. Your steadfast belief in me has been my anchor and my light.

For my beautiful children and grandchildren. You are the reason I dared to disrupt my default, the motivation behind every step I take toward growth and change. Your love fills my heart, your laughter fills my soul, and your presence makes my world infinitely brighter.

For my siblings. Though life shaped us in different ways and distance remains between us, my love for you remains too. The pieces of our past are woven into who I am, and for that, I hold nothing but gratitude.

# Foreword by Anika Apple

There is nothing more powerful than a mind made up.

Mea Brown is a force.

Her professional experience extends across CEOs and owners of multimillion-dollar organizations, governmental agencies, start-ups, and, of course, authors. She is a change agent for the change agents.

In this book, Mea presents the toolkit she has used to support full transformations in those whom she has advised and coached. As a gifted storyteller, Mea blends her personal experiences with the application of the mindset she unveils throughout the book. Mea's journey is one of marked transformation. Her story of overcoming adversity is incredibly powerful. She brings you fully into the moment with her, allowing you to experience the tension and conflicts as if they were your own. Before you know it, her words have brought you right back to the mirrored moments in your life with an invitation to now see yourself and make new decisions.

*Disrupt Your Default* delivers the true intent of the book. It brings you back to asking yourself if who you are being today is the version of yourself that you are actually choosing. From quiet decisions to bold and actionable steps that disrupt the status quo, Mea takes us through the journey to embrace our agency.

This book is filled with practical steps towards designing a rhythm of introspection. Mea highlights commonly experienced fears, battles with unworthiness and self-love, while empowering the reader by reminding them that they hold the pen to rewrite the stories of their lives. Every story leaves you wanting to know what happens next while offering you a moment to consider how to complete the story by creating the change you desire in your own life. It is like being given a gift to see yourself with fresh eyes in every chapter.

I have the honor of calling Mea a personal friend. Shortly after a consulting engagement, Mea and I experienced a divine connection. It was incredibly poignant. I knew that there would be some way that our work would connect us again. I remember praying after our call for the chance to work with Mea in some capacity. I recognized the immense talent across so many areas of business, but what struck me was her heart. I understood her ability to see opportunity and the ways in which her clients were unaware that they were the block to their own abundance or whatever they might have been seeking. Mea shared a couple of insights that cut right to the quick and helped me crystalize opportunities in my business.

Just over a year later, I was working on my first book. I was in prayer for the right editing partner, and I saw Mea's face. The beautiful reconnection led not only to her editing my book but also to a beautiful friendship that continues to bless my life. Mea has been a strategic coach for my business, my writing, and me personally. She helped me disrupt the patterns of procrastination that slowed my book's progress by addressing areas that needed healing. Mea helped me identify limiting beliefs that were impacting my business and supported me in shifting my mindset to receive the opportunities that began to flow. It was evident to me that her own experiences led her to some deep insights, along with her divine leading, that helped me through my transformation.

Mea Brown is a disruptor, brilliant storyteller, and muse. I invite you to take hold of the permission offered in this book. *Disrupt Your Default* calls you forward into becoming the person you truly want to be. It inspires you to live the life of your dreams. This book is the starting point you need to see yourself differently.

As a Trusted Advisor and coach, I've seen firsthand the power of transformation. I know that you possess the same potential. Let this book guide you. Let it be your compass as it guides you to the discovery of your true self.

Of all the things that need disruption, there is no calling more important than that which asks you to look within.

It is time for the best version of you to step forward.
This book reminds you that the freedom to change is in your own hands.

—Anika Apple

# Foreword by Nicole R. Itule-Busboom

Disrupt your default is a journey of self-discovery and personal growth. In this book, Mea Brown gives the reader not just a collection of words, but a guide to unlocking the potential within you. By opening herself up and sharing some deeply personal challenges, she reminds us that life is an ever-changing landscape, filled with challenges and opportunities, and this book aims to equip you with the tools to navigate it successfully.

In these pages, you will find insights, and strategies that will help you transform your life. Whether you are seeking to enhance your career, improve your relationships, or simply find a greater sense of peace and fulfillment, the principles shared here are designed to empower you to take control of your destiny.

As you embark on this journey, remember that change begins with a single step. Embrace the wisdom and exercises provided and allow yourself to grow and evolve. The path to a better you starts right here, and I am honored to be a part of the transformation with you.

Nicole R Itule-Busboom

# Introduction

## Why This Book Matters, And Why Now

This book doesn't matter because I'm an expert. It matters because I've lived it. Because I've walked through the things I'm writing about, and I've found a way to make my life better by disrupting my default. It matters because it's a part of me. Woven into who I am. Shaped by everything I've fought to unlearn, reclaim, and redefine.

I don't believe that every piece of our past, our present, or our future needs to be shared with the world. I am, by nature, a private person. Writing this book took courage. Not just because I had to relive parts of my story, but because my story overlaps with others. And I wanted to be intentional about what I shared, how I shared it, and when.

So why now? Because the timing is right. Because I had to live through it before I could write about it. Because it took time to find the right words to articulate what was happening beneath the surface, to name the patterns, and to understand the shifts I was making. And because I know there are people out there, maybe even you, who have struggled for a long time with who they are, where they are, and how to create the real change they've been dreaming about.

I don't claim to have all the answers. This book isn't exhaustive. It's not the full story or the only way. It's just some of it. Just a start.

If sharing my story helps even one person take that first step toward disrupting their default, then every word was worth it.

## Before and After: The Turning Point

For a long time, I believed struggle was the only road available to me. No matter how hard I tried or how much I longed for something different, life felt like a battle I could never win. My past weighed on me, shaping how I saw myself and what I believed was possible. I wasn't just surviving. I was stuck. Convinced that pain was all I would ever know. That joy was reserved for other people.

**But what if I was wrong?**

**What if the struggle wasn't the full story?**
**What if I had the power to disrupt everything I thought I knew and create something different?**

I didn't have the words for it at the time, but looking back, I can see that what I needed, what I had to do, was disrupt my default. Disrupt the patterns, the beliefs, the expectations I had simply accepted as my reality. The life I was living wasn't the only life available to me. But I had to be willing to question it first.

My journey through life has been anything but easy. It's been marked by both pain and resilience, heartbreak and healing. It has been a story of hurt, fear, sadness, shame, and hopelessness. But also one of love, joy, pride, success, and gratitude. Looking back, I see a clear divide. The life I lived before I gained the courage to disrupt my default, and the life I began to build after I made that choice.

In the before, I was afraid for others to see where I came from and who I used to be. I was ashamed. That fear and shame held me back from truly living and kept me locked in cycles of doubt and silence.

But sitting here today, in the after, I'm proud to say that I am no longer ashamed. I might have some regret, but not shame.

I've come to the conclusion that my past, while painful, holds value. Not just for me, but for anyone searching for proof that change is possible. Change isn't about rejecting who we were or where we came from. It's about choosing who we become and where we are going.

Not everything in my life needed to be different. But the parts shaped by pain, by fear, and by outdated patterns that no longer served me? Those needed to shift. And when I finally allowed myself to make those changes, I realized I wasn't just letting go of the past; I was making room for the future.

Yet, for years, I didn't know how to begin.

## The Struggle Before the Shift

I've made choices I'm not proud of and choices I want to high-five myself for making. I've felt love so deep it left me breathless, and I've felt the sting of betrayal from people I never thought would leave. I've been abandoned at my most vulnerable. And I've also, in my own ways, hurt people too.

Life has been messy, complicated, and full of lessons I never asked for. It's also been beautiful. And, in many ways, good to me. Both, and. Life has been both a struggle and a joy.

Real joy started showing up when I learned that I didn't have to keep carrying the pain of my past or the outdated beliefs about who I am and what's possible for me. It started showing up when I realized I could take what had shaped me and use it. Not as a life sentence, but as a foundation to build something new.

Let me be clear, this is not a book about being a victim.
It's not about weakness.
It's not about entitlement.

And, it's certainly not an excuse to stop showing up for yourself, for your family, for your friends, for your life.

This book is about how we reckon with the pieces of our past that have shaped us. Especially the ones that left deep imprints on who we are. For some, that may mean navigating trauma that shattered their sense of self. For others, it might be the slow erosion of confidence, the weight of expectations, or the quiet ache of feeling unseen. Disrupting your default isn't about measuring pain or comparing scars. It's about reclaiming the parts of yourself that life tried to rewrite.

And let me say this again, this is not a book that says, *Oh, I'm so sorry for you, you poor thing.*

Because that's not what you need.

This book is also not a permission slip to sit back and say, *I've been hurt, so I don't have to try.* That's not what you deserve. This book is about choice. About ownership. About deciding fully and completely that you are going to create the life you want, no matter what has come before.

Because if you're anything like me, the struggles you've faced didn't just break you. They built you. They made you a fighter. They made you stronger, wiser, faster. They thickened your skin, sharpened your instincts, and taught you to work harder. And for that, in a way, I am thankful.

But being strong isn't enough. Surviving isn't enough.

At some point, I had to ask myself: *What kind of life do I actually want to live?*

It wasn't just about being tough. It was about becoming the best version of myself. Not just for me, but for my husband, my children, my grandchildren, my friends, and the legacy I will leave behind.

And to do that, some things had to change.

I had to learn to love myself. Not in a surface-level, self-care-routine kind of way. But in a deep, unshakable way.
I had to set boundaries, not just with others, but with my own patterns of thinking.
I had to stop seeing the world as a harsh, unrelenting place and start

seeing the good that was still out there.

I had to shift my mindset. Not into toxic positivity, but into something real, something balanced, something that honored both my strength and my softness.

And that's what this book is about.

It's about balance.
It's about learning how to heal without losing the fire.
It's about changing your life while holding onto the parts of yourself that made you unstoppable.

And if you're ready to do that, really do that, then you're in the right place.

## Let This Book Meet You Where You Are

This isn't a book you have to read in order, and it's certainly not a rigid set of instructions. It's an offering of stories, reflections, and insights that might challenge you, encourage you, or meet you exactly where you need them most.

Some days, you may want to sit with a chapter and let it settle in. Other days, you may just need a simple reminder that you're not alone in this. Either way, I hope these pages serve as a steady hand on your shoulder. A gentle nudge forward. A reminder that you are capable of creating the extraordinary life you desire.

As you move through this book, you may notice that some concepts could have been combined, or that there is an overlap between certain ideas. That's intentional. Some lessons need to be revisited from different angles before they fully take root. And sometimes, **hearing**

**a familiar idea in a new way is exactly what we need to create lasting change.**

Throughout the book and at the end, you'll find journal prompts and questions designed to help you reflect more deeply and take these ideas beyond the page. There are no right or wrong answers. Just space to explore, to question, and to discover what's possible for you.

Let yourself engage with this book in whatever way feels natural. Read what speaks to you. Leave what doesn't. Come back when you need to.

And, most of all, trust that you are already on your way.

# Part 1

Rethink – Challenging the Life You Were Given

Shadow Scribe Media

# Chapter One

---

# The Life I Had.
# The Life I
# Wanted.

*"Scars remind us where we've been. They don't have to dictate where we're going."*
**— David Rossi (*Criminal Minds*)**

### Growing Up Too Soon

S ome people ease into adulthood. I crashed into it. Maturity wasn't a choice. It was survival.

When I should have been playing, I was planning. When I should have been dreaming, I was calculating. Always watching. Always figuring out how to stay safe, how to keep my siblings safe, how to make sure we had enough. *Enough food. Enough money. Enough protection.*

I learned quickly that if I didn't take care of myself, no one else would. That kind of pressure doesn't just shape a person. It *hardens* them. It turns self-reliance into a weapon. It teaches you to solve every problem alone. To never ask for help. To believe that needing people is dangerous.

For years, I carried that belief. Even when my life changed. Even when I was married. Even when I had people who loved me. My instinct remained the same: *Solve the problem. Handle it alone. Don't ask.*

It took me years to see what that instinct was costing me.

## The Cost of Independence

Being independent kept me alive. It also made me hard in ways I never meant to be.

I wasn't cold, but sometimes I seemed like I was.
I wasn't cruel, but my words could be sharp.
I wasn't closed off, but I kept people at arm's length.

Not because I didn't love them, but because I was terrified.

Terrified of being misunderstood.
Terrified of being rejected.
Terrified that if I let someone in, they might leave.

So, I built walls. Walls made of silence. Of self-reliance. Of never showing weakness. And for years, I carried the weight of my past into every single part of my life.

## Survival Mode: The Weight of My Past

My life wasn't just hard. It was damn near unbearable.

For me, real danger wasn't a rare moment. It was *constant.* Survival wasn't a lesson I learned in my teens. It was the first thing I ever knew.

My mother was a teenager when she had me. A child raising a child, trapped in a violent relationship with little family support. The chaos she lived in became my normal.

And when I say I grew up fast, I don't mean I learned responsibility early. I mean, by the time I was seven, innocence was something I had already lost.

By then, I already knew what it meant to flinch when a hand was raised.
I already knew how to disappear into the background when danger was near.
I already understood things no child should have to understand.

The abuse my mother suffered didn't stop with her. And by the time my parents divorced when I was nine, the worst was still ahead.

## The Moment That Changed Everything

I remember standing on the porch with my siblings, staring down an impossible choice: *which parent do you want to live with?*

There were four of us. My baby sister stayed with my mother. My brother, the only boy, was sent to live with my abusive father.

And me?

I was the oldest. The protector. The one who felt like she had to take the hit if it meant someone else wouldn't. I stayed with my father, too. My other sister stayed with my mother to help care for the baby.

We were kids.
Separated.
Not by choice, but by necessity.

And what came next wasn't relief. It was an avalanche.

The abuse didn't stop. It *escalated*. And beyond my father's cruelty, there were others. His friends and other relatives. I learned that being invisible was the safest thing I could be. That silence was survival.

The guilt of not protecting my siblings followed me into adulthood. The shame of what happened lived in my bones. And for years, I carried it all like a weight I thought I would never put down.

## The Cost of Survival

By sixteen, I was on my own. High school, a pregnancy, and three part-time jobs filled my days. It was all I knew.

Survival had become my identity.

I worked harder than everyone around me.
I expected nothing from anyone.
I relied on no one.

And for a long time, I thought that was enough.

But something kept pulling at me. Tiny glimmers of light, showing up when I least expected them. A small kindness. A moment of peace. A fleeting sense of possibility.

For years, those moments felt too small to hold on to. But even when I couldn't fully believe in them, they never disappeared.

Hope lingered.

Even in my darkest moments, something in me whispered, *Maybe things could be different.*

## Breaking the Cycle

I thought my survival instincts were permanent. That the way I operated, the walls I built, the independence I clung to, and the weight I carried, was just *who I was.*

But what if it wasn't?

What if I wasn't stuck?
What if I had the power to rewrite my story?

Those questions were the beginning of something powerful for me.

I started to realize my beliefs weren't facts. That the things I told myself; *you have to do everything alone.* People *will always leave.* Struggle *is all there is,* weren't *truths.* They were just patterns.

Patterns I had the power to break.

I couldn't rewrite the past.
I couldn't erase the scars.

But I *could* decide what happened next.

So, I started questioning everything.

*Where did these beliefs come from?*
*Did they still serve me?*
*And most importantly, could I change them?*

The answer, in part, was *yes*.

Your past doesn't have to define your future.
Your struggles don't have to be your identity.
Your pain doesn't get the final say.

You are not bound to the patterns that broke you. You are not limited to the survival instincts that once kept you safe. You are capable of building a life beyond what you've known.

But before you can create something new, you have to ask yourself one hard question.

**What if the story you've been telling yourself isn't the whole truth?**

# Chapter Two

---

# What If I'm Wrong?

*"If you change the way you look at things, the things you look at change."*
— **Wayne Dyer**

This book is an invitation to rethink, reclaim, and redefine your life.

But before we can embrace change, we have to start by questioning the stories we've been telling ourselves. And let's be clear, questioning those stories doesn't mean forgetting what happened. It doesn't mean minimizing the pain or pretending the past didn't shape us. It means asking, *How much of my life today is still being shaped by things that are no longer happening?*

Sometimes, that means facing the hardest question of all.

**What if I'm wrong?**

What if I'm wrong about how I see my life today?

What if I'm making choices based on wounds instead of reality?

What if I'm living as though I'm still trapped, when I'm actually free?

Every decision we make, every belief we hold, is shaped, sometimes subtly, sometimes profoundly, by the pieces of our past that brought us here. For me, that was undeniably true. As I mentioned in the introduction, my story didn't just shape how I saw the world. It shaped how I saw *myself*.

*Past tense.*

Because I no longer see myself the way I once did. I have rewritten and redefined what my life means. What I'm capable of. And who I choose to be.

But back then? Back then, survival wasn't just a skill, it was all I knew.

I didn't just *learn* resilience. I *lived* it. Every single day felt like a battle. I wasn't just reacting to the world. I was bracing for impact. Always expecting the worst.

The challenges I faced weren't just external. They took root deep inside me. They shaped the way I saw myself. They shaped the way I saw the world.

And because I mostly believed the world was a cold, unrelenting place, I wrapped myself in armor built from pain.

Those beliefs once shielded me.

At least, that's what I thought.

But they didn't just protect me.

**They trapped me.**

They shaped the lens through which I saw everything.

They convinced me that the world was dark, that people couldn't be trusted, and that hope was a luxury for others.

For years, I accepted that as truth.

I believed my life would always be hard. That struggle was my reality. That nothing would ever change.

I thought I had drawn the short stick in some cosmic lottery, and that I was on this earth to endure, not to thrive.

And because I believed that, **I lived it.**

## The Lies I Refused to Keep Living

I accepted things into my life that never should have been accepted.

I accepted *abuse* as an adult because that's what I had known as a child. It never occurred to me that love could be anything other than pain. So I stayed in relationships far longer than I ever should have. I tolerated things I never should have.

I accepted *unwanted advances* from men in the workplace because I didn't think I had the right to say no. I assumed my value was **transactional**, measured by what others wanted from me, not by who I was.

I accepted *constant chaos* from people who drained me, because I believed it was my role to absorb their pain, and solve their problems while never acknowledging my own.

I endured *feelings of unworthiness*. I told myself I wasn't good enough. That I didn't come from the right family, have the right background, or belong in the right circles. I convinced myself that success, happiness, and even peace were for people who had earned them in ways I never could.

I accepted that I would never be more than how people saw me.

That the girl they pitied, the girl who barely made it out, was the only version of me that could ever exist.

But they never saw the battle inside me. They never saw how hard I was fighting, not just to survive, but to *break free*.

The problem was, I didn't know how to separate the two.

I wanted something different, but I was still holding onto the very beliefs that kept me stuck.

So, I endured.

I endured the circumstances *others* created for me.
I endured the ones *I* unknowingly created for myself.
I endured because I didn't know anything else.

But endurance is not the same as *living*.

And deep down, I knew something else was waiting for me.

## The Question That Changed Everything

As I got older, something inside me started to shift.

A quiet voice within me, one that had been silenced for years, began to rise.

At first, it was barely a whisper, buried beneath the weight of everything I had been through.

But over time, it grew stronger.

Daring to challenge the story I had clung to for so long.

Until one day, I finally stopped. I took a breath. And I started listening.

That was the day I asked myself the question that *shook the foundation of everything I thought I knew.*

### What if I was wrong?

What if I had spent my entire life looking through a lens that was distorted?

What if the limits I had accepted were never real?

What if the story I had been telling myself wasn't the whole truth?

That question lingered at the edges of my mind, surfacing now and then. But I never truly sat with it until one moment changed everything.

That day was profoundly hard.

I was sitting alone at my kitchen table, a cup of coffee in my hands, the unbearable weight of my own existence pressing down on me. And the thought crept in, unbidden.

*What's the point?*

*Why does any of this matter?*

The surrounding silence was deafening. But within it, something surfaced. A small, quiet, *revolutionary* question.

What if I had the power to rewrite them?

Because every belief we hold started as a story.

Some were given to us. Others, we crafted ourselves. Some empower us. Others keep us small.

And the most dangerous ones?

They're the ones we never question.

It's time to change that.

# Chapter Three

---

# Rewriting the Narrative

*"We do not see things as they are, we see them as we are."*
**— Anaïs Nin**

E very story we tell ourselves is built on a belief.

And every belief has the power to either expand our world or shrink it.

Beliefs are not just thoughts we have; they are the invisible architects of our lives. They guide our choices, shape our relationships, and color how we see the world. Some are empowering. Others?

They keep us stuck in cycles we were never meant to stay in.

And the most dangerous thing about beliefs is that we don't always realize when they're running the show.

They become so deeply ingrained, woven from experience, shaped by pain, and reinforced by fear, that we rarely pause to examine them.

We accept them as truths, when in reality, they might just be outdated stories that no longer serve us.

**And that's the key.**

If Beliefs are stories, they can be rewritten.

Not ignored. Not erased. But redefined.

**Because when we rewrite our beliefs, we rewrite our lives.**

## The Stories We Carry

Beliefs are built over time. They aren't formed in a single moment. They are stitched together through experiences, environments, and the voices of people who influenced us. Sometimes for the better, sometimes for the worse.

And before we know it, we stop questioning them.

But if we want to grow, we have to make a conscious choice to do just that. To evaluate, challenge, and rewrite the beliefs that no longer align with the life we are building.

This work isn't easy. It requires honesty. It demands courage. It asks us to be vulnerable enough to admit that some of the things we've held onto for so long might not actually be true.

And that's uncomfortable.

But living a life shaped by outdated beliefs that keep us small is more uncomfortable.

## The Weight of Old Beliefs

Some beliefs are powerful allies.

When they are rooted in hope, love, and joy; they encourage us to take chances, embrace opportunities, and build meaningful connections.

But when they stem from fear, pain, or insecurity; they distort our view of what's possible.

They tether us to past versions of ourselves that no longer fit.

I want you to pause for a moment.

Think about it.

How many of your daily thoughts or reactions stem from beliefs you formed years ago?

Maybe it's the belief that the world is harsh and unforgiving, A belief born from a difficult chapter of your life, but no longer reflective of where you are today.

Or maybe it's the quiet but persistent thought that you're not good enough. A belief shaped by a single painful rejection, yet still echoing in your mind years later.

I know this because I've lived it.

For years, I carried beliefs that weighed me down. Beliefs forged in moments when survival was my only goal. At the time, those beliefs served me. They gave me structure in chaos, helped me make sense of an overwhelming world, and protected me when I needed it most.

But eventually they stopped being armor and became chains.

They kept me from trusting.

From seeing possibilities.

From recognizing my own power.

And the most dangerous thing about them?

They felt like absolute truths.

That's the tricky thing about beliefs.

We don't just think them.

We live them.

We repeat them to ourselves until they become ingrained in the foundation of our reality.

But the reality is, beliefs are not always truths.

Sometimes, they are just stories.

Stories shaped by pain. Stories built in moments of fear. Stories that once protected us but are now keeping us from the life we deserve.

And like any story...

They can be rewritten.

Rewriting your beliefs doesn't mean dismissing your past or denying the lessons it taught you.

It means honoring what those beliefs once did for you while recognizing that they don't have to define your future.

It means asking yourself the hard questions.

***Is this belief helping me grow?***

***Is it empowering me?***

***Or is it keeping me small, stuck, or afraid?***

This process can feel daunting. It's kind of like walking into a cluttered room where every item carries a memory. But with patience and intention, you can begin to clear the space.

Hold each belief up to the light and ask yourself:

Does this still belong here?

For me, the shift began with a single, uncomfortable question.

***What if I'm wrong?***

*What if the belief that the world is inherently hostile isn't true?*

*What if my pain, while valid, isn't the whole story?*

Those questions were unsettling. They challenged the foundation of how I saw the world. But they also cracked open the door to something I had never fully considered.

What if I could believe something better?

Your Beliefs. Your Choice.

Change doesn't happen overnight.

Rewriting deeply held beliefs is a process.

It's a series of small, deliberate steps.

It's about collecting new evidence, rewriting old narratives, and sitting with the discomfort of uncertainty.

But with every step forward, the weight of limiting beliefs begins to lift. Replaced by a growing sense of freedom, empowerment, and hope.

So, I invite you to pause and reflect.

What beliefs are shaping your life right now?

Are they helping you move forward, or are they holding you back?

Are they rooted in truth, or are they relics of a past you've outgrown?

Beliefs are powerful. But they are not permanent.

And once you start rewriting the beliefs that have shaped you, something else begins to happen.

You start noticing the rules.

Not the ones written in books, but the ones that live in the spaces between expectation and reality. The ones that tell you who you're allowed to be, how much space you're allowed to take up, and what dreams are "realistic."

But what if those rules weren't meant for you?

*The power to change your life begins with the courage to change your mind.*

# Chapter Four

---

# Breaking the Rules

*"Every time you break a rule, you are opening the door to new possibilities."*

**—Terry Pratchett**

S ome rules are written in ink. Others are written in silence.

Not the ones enforced by laws or taught in classrooms, but the unspoken ones that dictate how you show up in the world. The quiet rules that shape your choices, define your limits, and decide which dreams are deemed "realistic."

The ones that whisper, this is just how things are.

For most of my life, I didn't question the rules. I didn't even recognize them for what they were. I had carried them for so long they felt like part of me.

**Until one day, they didn't.**

That's when I started asking the hard questions:

*Who decided how ambitious I was allowed to be before it became too much?*

*Who decided my worth was measured by how much I gave to others while ignoring myself?*

*Who decided that silence was safer than speaking up?*

I didn't make those rules. Yet, I had been living by them.

And I know I'm not alone in this.

We all feel it. That unspoken pressure to always put others first. To shrink ourselves into what is expected. To believe ambition is unbecoming or that we should be grateful for what we have instead of daring to want more.

These rules don't have to be written down to be real. If you've ever felt their weight, you know exactly what I mean.

**But, rules are not permanent.**

**Rules are not sacred.**

They were created by people.

And anything created can be undone.

So I started undoing.

## Challenging the Status Quo

The first step was recognizing the rules that had shaped me. The next was deciding which ones had to go.

And let me be clear about this. I didn't grow up in a world where questioning the status quo was encouraged.

It was actively discouraged.

I was raised in a time and place where obedience was safer. Questioning anything; authority, tradition, "the way things have always been", was unheard of.

Families kept secrets.

Communities operated within their own unwritten rules, and people were expected to fall in line without question.

That was my world. That was the paradigm I was born into.

I was taught that fitting in mattered more than thinking for myself. That children were to be seen and not heard. That adults were always right, and "the way things are" was just the way things are.

So I didn't question it. **I tried to follow the rules.**

And there was a strange kind of safety in that.

If I didn't stand out, I couldn't be criticized.

If I went along with things, I wouldn't rock the boat.

And if I didn't rock the boat, maybe, just maybe, I wouldn't make things worse.

But the thing about *silence* is,

*It doesn't keep you safe.*

It keeps you **stuck**.

I didn't realize that until I started questioning why I felt so suffocated. Why staying quiet and staying small no longer felt safe.

The silence I once relied on had turned into something else.

Something heavy.

Something I could no longer carry.

So I started listening to myself.

At first, it was just a whisper: This isn't right.

But that whisper grew louder.

And louder.

Until I could no longer pretend that the life I had was the life I wanted.

## Breaking the Cycle

The first place I challenged the status quo wasn't at work or in a public space.

It was in my own home.

I started noticing how these invisible rules had slipped into how I was raising my own children. Without realizing it, I had been passing down the same expectations:

**Obedience over questioning.**

**Silence over self-expression.**

**Blending in over standing out.**

And that? That didn't sit right with me.

I wanted something different for them.

So I started making small shifts. Encouraging curiosity instead of shutting it down. Allowing tough conversations instead of avoiding them. Letting my kids express themselves in ways I never had the chance to.

**It wasn't perfect. I failed a lot. Sometimes I caught myself repeating the very patterns I was trying to break.**

But I reminded myself often;

I am breaking a cycle.

I am creating change.

Not just for myself, but for them.

**And that felt right. Even when it was hard.**

## The Price of Being Different

And let me tell you, it didn't go unnoticed.

The more I challenged the old ways, the more resistance I faced. Especially from family. They didn't understand why I was trying to do things differently, and truthfully, they didn't want to understand.

Because acknowledging my choices would mean facing their own.

So instead of support, I got criticism.

They saw my parenting choices as a rejection of theirs.

They called my refusal to use fear and control soft parenting.

They told me I was raising kids who would never survive in the real world.

But they didn't see what I saw.

They didn't see that I wasn't trying to tear them down. I was just trying to build something better.

And if that made them uncomfortable, so be it.

Because cycles don't break themselves.

Someone has to be willing to take the criticism. *That was me.*

Someone has to be willing to bear the discomfort of being different. *That was me.*

Someone has to choose growth over acceptance, even when it costs them belonging. *That was me.*

Someone has to have the courage to question the rules, rewrite them, and create a different future.

And that?

**That is you, too.**

Because rules only hold power when we refuse to question them.

And once I started questioning the rules imposed on me, I realized something even bigger.

The most limiting rules weren't just the ones society had handed me.

They were the ones I had accepted as the truth.

Not just about what I was allowed to do, but about who I was allowed to be.

And that's when I saw it clearly;

It wasn't just the external rules that kept me small. It was my **own beliefs.** The silent, internal rules I had carried for years.

The belief that struggle was just my reality.
The belief that I was stuck, incapable of change.
The belief that who I was would always be who I had to be.

But what if that wasn't true either?

What if the biggest limits weren't the ones put on me?
But the ones I had put on myself?

# Chapter Five

---

# From Fixed to Free

*"Becoming is better than being."*
— **Carol Dweck**

I spent years breaking free from external rules, and at first, I didn't realize the ones inside me were just as powerful.

For most of my life, I believed things just were the way they were.

If something was hard today, it would still be hard tomorrow.

If I struggled, I would always struggle.

If life had been unfair, then fairness wasn't meant for me.

I believed my experiences, my circumstances, and my hardships were set in stone.

I never questioned that belief.

And because I never questioned it, I lived it.

I carried frustration, anger, and resentment for years.

I was angry at life for being unfair. I was angry at the world for being harsh. I was angry at other people who seemed to have it easier.

I had no interest in seeing my struggles as opportunities to grow.

Why would I? I hadn't chosen them.

How could they be anything other than burdens?

I felt stuck. Trapped by beliefs I didn't even realize were holding me back. The idea of questioning them, of rethinking them entirely, felt impossible.

I didn't know where to start.

And I certainly didn't understand that my mindset was playing a key role in shaping my reality.

## The Power of Mindset

Beliefs lay the foundation of our lives.

But mindset determines how we build upon it.

Think of your mindset as the operating system of your thoughts. Always running in the background, shaping how you interpret experiences, challenges, and possibilities.

And while mindset is often framed as a simple choice between two categories; fixed or growth, the reality is much deeper than that.

Mindset exists on a spectrum, shifting and evolving based on our self-awareness, experiences, and willingness to challenge old patterns.

## Fixed vs. Growth Mindset

At one end of the spectrum is a fixed mindset. Rigid, resistant, and rooted in the belief that things are the way they are and cannot change.

A fixed mindset tells you:

You either have it or you don't.

If you're not good at something now, you never will be.

You are who you are. Take it or leave it.

Failure means stop trying.

It clings to the idea that your abilities, intelligence, and circumstances are unchangeable.

It convinces you that taking risks isn't worth it. That your potential is capped. That trying and failing is worse than not trying at all.

When paired with limiting beliefs, a fixed mindset can feel like a trap, locking you into old patterns and preventing you from even considering a different path.

At the other end of the spectrum is a growth mindset. Adaptive, resilient, and rooted in the belief that challenges are stepping stones, not roadblocks.

A growth mindset tells you:

I can learn and improve.

Challenges make me stronger.

Failure is just data, and I can use it to grow.

This is hard right now, but I can figure it out.

It doesn't ignore difficulties. It reframes them.

It whispers: *"This isn't the end of the story. Keep going."*

And in that whisper, it invites transformation.

## Mindset in Action: A Personal Shift

For me, adopting a growth mindset wasn't an overnight revelation.

It wasn't a lesson someone taught me.

I didn't grow up seeing examples of what it looked like.

For most of my life, I didn't even realize mindset was a choice.

I just knew I wanted something different.

For years, I reinforced the belief that struggle was just life.

That hardship was something I had to live with, not learn from.

That my circumstances were something to endure, not change.

And because I believed that, I stayed stuck.

Not because I wanted to be, but because I didn't know how to be anything else.

I don't remember the exact day when that belief changed.

I don't remember what triggered it.

But I do remember the moment when I caught myself saying six simple words.

***"This is just the way I am."***

It hit me like a punch to the gut.

I had said it without thinking, as if it were an undeniable truth.

And then, just as quickly, another thought followed.

**But what if that isn't true?**

What if the way I am today isn't the way I always have to be? What if I could change? Even just a little.

That single question cracked something open inside of me.

Because if I could be wrong about that, what else could I be wrong about?

So I started testing the theory.

Instead of assuming I wasn't capable, I started experimenting.

I had spent my entire life believing I wasn't smart enough. That I wasn't good at certain things because I didn't come from the right family, or have the right education. That I wasn't the kind of person who could speak in public. That I wasn't disciplined enough to follow through. That I wasn't strong enough to say no to things that drained me. That I wasn't worthy of more than what I had been given.

For years, I avoided what felt uncomfortable.

I walked away from conversations when they felt hard. I shut down when I was frustrated. I ran when I was hurt.

And without realizing it, I was reinforcing the very patterns that were keeping me from what I wanted most.

So instead of labeling myself as "bad" at something, I tried something different.

I forced myself to have hard conversations instead of shutting down. I resisted the urge to run and instead stood in discomfort. I started setting boundaries, even when they felt foreign.

I didn't change overnight.

There were missteps. There was doubt.

But slowly, I started collecting proof that growth wasn't just possible,

It was already happening.

## Rewriting Limiting Beliefs

A fixed mindset tells you:

This is just how life is.

A growth mindset asks:

What can I learn from this, and how can I grow?

That single shift in perspective changes everything.

It opens the door to curiosity and possibility.

Changing my mindset was the first step. But what came next was the real challenge. Because changing beliefs is one thing, living them is another. I had spent years believing struggle was my reality. Now, I had to choose something different. Something that felt almost radical.

I had to choose hope. Hope that change wasn't only possible, but that it was mine to create.

# Chapter Six

---

# Hope Is A Rebellion

## The Power of Choosing Positivity

*"The greatest weapon against stress is our ability to choose one thought over another."*

**—William James**

H ope is a choice. Positivity is a choice. And for a long time, I didn't think I had the right to choose either.

On the surface, positivity seemed simple to me. In reality, it was one of the hardest tools I had to learn to use.

It is easy to dismiss hope as naïve, as if choosing to see possibility means ignoring pain. But real hope is about choosing where to place my focus, even in the midst of the hardest moments. It's about shaping my mindset, rewiring my thoughts, and navigating life with hope and a positive outlook. Even when everything in me wants to shut down.

I know, for some people, just hearing the word positivity triggers an eye roll.

We've all been there. Someone saying, *"Just think positive!"* at the worst possible moment. As if flipping a mental switch could make all of our problems disappear. That kind of forced, sugar-coated positivity feels dismissive, unrealistic, and honestly? Downright annoying.

But I'm not talking about that kind of positivity.

Real positivity isn't about pretending everything's okay. It's about choosing where to focus my energy.

Even in my hardest seasons, I realized I had a choice.

I could stay stuck in fear, frustration, and hopelessness.

Or I could look for what was good, what was possible, and what was within my control.

Positivity wasn't about denying my reality. It was about creating space for hope.

Because while I couldn't always control what was happening to me, I could always control how I responded. And my response was my power.

## From Fear to Possibility

For the most part, I'm naturally a **glass-half-full kind of person.**

But that wasn't always true.

You've read this far, so you know a little about my story. You know, there were days when everything felt impossible, heavy, and hard. Days when I braced myself for the worst. Waiting for the other shoe to drop. Convinced that any moment of happiness was just a setup for the next disaster.

Because when you've been abandoned, abused, and hurt, it shapes how you see yourself.

It teaches you to expect disappointment.

And even when there was a bright side, I struggled to see it.

Then, during a particularly dark season of my life, I had a conversation with a friend that shifted my perspective.

Maddie and I had spent years raising our kids together. Our friendship had formed over coffee-fueled conversations while our children played. And to me, Maddie's life was perfect.

She had the sweet Southern roots. The well-to-do family. The picture-perfect life. At least, that's how it looked from the outside.

But as we grew closer, she started opening up. And I learned Maddie struggled, too.

Maybe they weren't the same as mine, but behind closed doors, she carried pain and challenges of her own.

One day, after she shared something particularly difficult, I finally asked,

*"Maddie, how do you stay so positive all the time?"*

She smiled, shook her head, and said,

*"I'm not always positive. I get angry. I get frustrated. I get sad. But I just refuse to let those feelings take over."*

And that moment was eye opening for me.

Because I wanted that.

I wanted to face life's struggles without letting them consume me.

I wanted to choose positivity, not just when things were easy, but especially when they weren't.

So I started practicing and chasing positivity, even when it felt hard.

And I quickly learned that positivity isn't a one-time decision. It's a daily choice.

Some days, an hourly choice.

And like with anything, the more practiced, the easier it became.

## Finding the Good. Even in the Hard.

For me, learning to choose positivity wasn't about ignoring my struggles. The hard stuff still came.

It just meant I started looking at it differently.

I started facing the storm and saying:

*"I can handle this. I will get through this."*

And I did.

One of the biggest lessons Maddie taught me was that I didn't have to control everything. I just had to control how I responded.

Life was always going to bring a few difficulties. Some would be small. Some would be enormous. But the one thing that was always within my control was my response.

## My Mindset. My Response. My Next Step Forward.

So when things started feeling overwhelming, I stopped and asked myself,

*"What can I control right now?"*

Sometimes, the only answer was taking a deep breath.

Or writing my thoughts down instead of letting them spiral.

Or choosing just one thing that would help me feel grounded.

Positivity wasn't about fixing everything at once. It was about finding one piece of solid ground to stand on and place my hope in.

## Rewriting the Internal Dialogue

For years, I carried old, familiar thoughts.

**"You're not good enough."**
**"Nothing ever works out for you."**

I didn't just think about those things; I believed them. They weren't fleeting doubts; they were embedded truths, shaping how I saw myself and my future.

It never occurred to me that I could challenge them.

But I could.

And so can you.

Instead of letting those thoughts dictate my reality, I started paying attention to them. I noticed when they showed up. I noticed how quickly they arrived, and how easily I accepted them. And once I noticed them, I did something radical. I questioned them.

Instead of "Nothing ever works out for me," I asked myself,

**"Is that really true? Or have I just been focusing on everything that's gone wrong instead of what's gone right?"**

Instead of "I'll never be good enough," I asked,

**"What if the only thing standing between me and my growth is the story I keep telling myself?"**

This wasn't about forcing myself to be positive all the time. It was about making space for the possibility that my old beliefs weren't the full truth.

And I found out that the more I challenged those thoughts, the weaker they became.

The more I leaned into **hope,** the more it expanded.

Positivity isn't about ignoring struggle. It's about deciding that struggle won't have the final say.

Every day, we have a choice. We can either reinforce old narratives or to step into something new.

Hope is the choice to believe that something new is possible, even when it feels impossible.

## The Ripple Effect of Positivity

Positivity also taught me to celebrate the small wins.

When everything felt heavy, when progress felt invisible, I looked for something good, even if it was small.

And the more I practiced seeing the possibilities instead of the roadblocks, the more my entire world started to shift.

I became more hopeful in uncertainty.

I started choosing resilience over defeat.

And, maybe most surprising of all is these changes affected everyone around me.

Positivity and hope don't just shift your mindset.

They become contagious.

## Your Turn

Every morning, I remind myself:

*"I have a choice."*

I can carry joy with me, even in the hardest moments.

I can choose to see the good.

And when I do?

I become a source of light for others, too.

So let me ask you:

What does choosing positivity look like for you?

Maybe it's shifting how you talk to yourself.

Maybe it's taking one step forward, no matter how small.

Maybe it's simply noticing something beautiful that you've over-looked before.

Positivity doesn't mean hardships disappear.

It means you find the strength to navigate them in a different way.

Choosing positivity and hoping for the best possible outcome shifted my perspective. But I needed something more. I needed something that would help me break free from the deeply ingrained beliefs that kept pulling me back. I needed a way to retrain my mind to stop accepting old narratives and to start embracing new ones.

What I didn't realize at the time was that my brain was already lis-tening. And every thought I repeated, every word I told myself, was shaping the way I saw the world, and myself.

## Chapter Seven

# Your Brain is Listening. What Are You Telling It?

*"Words are, of course, the most powerful drug used by mankind."*
— **Rudyard Kipling**

O nce I started truly understanding what was going on inside me, I knew I needed more help. I needed tools. Tools to help me grow. Tools to help me become the fullest version of myself.

This process I was going through wasn't about erasing my past, because that's not possible. It was about acknowledging where I'd been, what I believed, owning where I was, and being intentional about shaping where I was going.

So, to help with this process, I did what I do best. I read.

Books have always been my teachers. My mentors. My guides. I learn best by diving in, absorbing, and exploring different perspectives. And that's exactly what I did. I devoured books on self-reflection, growth, and transformation. And somewhere along the way, someone handed me a treasured book. A small, unassuming book filled with scriptures, affirmations, and quotes.

I don't remember the title. I wish I did. It meant so much to me for so long, and somehow, in the chaos of life, I misplaced it.

But I remember the impact.

The scriptures? Familiar. Comforting. The quotes? Insightful. Encouraging.

But the affirmations?

They got me.

And at first, not in a good way.

I read them and thought, This is ridiculous.

"You're doing great today." *(No, I'm not.)*
"You are worthy and capable." *(Not really.)*
"You are strong." *(I don't feel strong.)*

It felt forced. Fake. Like meaningless words meant to trick me into believing something I knew wasn't true.

But I kept coming back to them. Not because I believed them, but because something about them challenged me.

And over time, I realized something important.

Affirmations aren't about faking positivity or magically making life better just by saying nice things to yourself.

They are about shifting how we think. About moving from where we are to where we want to be.

And that mattered because, at that point in my journey, I was stuck.

I was spending so much time questioning, deconstructing, and untangling my past that I had fallen into a cycle of ruminating. Replaying what had gone wrong. Focusing on what was broken. Sitting in the weight of what I lacked.

And while all of that was work I needed to do, I couldn't stay there forever.

Rethinking your life is powerful, but it can also keep you trapped if you don't take the next steps of reframing and reshaping your beliefs and thoughts.

And that's where affirmations started to help.

## Reframing My Thoughts

When I first started using affirmations, I was skeptical.

And not just me. Other people in my life were skeptical, too.

I remember bringing up affirmations in a conversation with some women from my church circle, women I deeply respected. And almost immediately, it turned into a debate.

Some dismissed affirmations as wishful thinking. Others told me I was shifting the focus away from faith and onto myself.

And in that moment, I didn't know how to respond. Because the truth is, I was still figuring it out for myself.

But what I've learned since then is that affirmations are not about pretending life is perfect.

They're not about ignoring faith or replacing it with self-reliance.

They're about creating a new dialogue with ourselves.

A dialogue that is kinder, more intentional, and more empowering than the one we've carried for years.

At their core, affirmations are simply positive statements, full of hope, designed to challenge and reshape our thoughts.

They serve as reminders of who we are becoming, what we deserve, and the beliefs we are choosing to step into.

And this part was huge for me. There is actual science to back them up.

Our brains are constantly evolving through neuroplasticity, which means every thought we repeat strengthens a particular neural pathway, much like carving a trail through a forest. The more we think a certain way, the more automatic those thoughts become.

Affirmations helped me **redirect my mind away from fear and doubt and toward confidence, peace, and self-belief.**

Think about it like this:

Have you ever found yourself humming along to a song you don't even like, just because it played everywhere?

That song for me was *Shake It Off,* by Taylor Swift. I didn't love it. I didn't hate it. But I knew every word, simply because it played everywhere when it first came out.

That's the power of repetition.

Affirmations work the same way. Except instead of letting negativity take root, I started using repetition to reinforce beliefs that empowered me.

But I've also learned that saying the words isn't enough.

**I had to believe them.**

**I had to act on them.**

**I had to let them shape the way I moved through the world.**

Because saying "I am confident and capable" means nothing if I avoid challenges.

Saying "I deserve love and respect" is empty if I continue allowing people to mistreat me.

The real shift happens when belief and action align.

## Beyond the Words

For me, affirmations became like planting seeds.

Saying the words was the first step, but the action I took, how I nurtured those beliefs, how I let them take root, was what made them real.

I also had to learn that affirmations alone weren't enough.

The words we say to ourselves matter.

But so does the way we choose to see the world.

Because what good is speaking words of strength and encouragement if I spend the rest of my day looking for proof that they aren't true?

What good is saying, "I am growing and learning" if I immediately shut down every opportunity to learn something new?

Affirmations are also not about blind optimism. They are about choosing to see possibility even in the midst of struggle.

Choosing, even in difficult moments, to focus on what's possible instead of what's missing.

Because if I've learned anything on this journey, it's this:

**Our words shape our thoughts.**

**Our thoughts shape our actions.**

**And our actions shape the life we build.**

So we don't just say it once.

We say it until we believe it.

We say it until it becomes second nature.

We say it until it's not just words, but truth.

And when we do?

We start to see the world and the life we are living differently.

# Part 2

Reclaim – Taking Ownership of Who You Are

Shadow Scribe Media

# Chapter Eight

---

# Seeing Yourself Clearly

*"Knowing yourself is the beginning of all wisdom."*

— **Aristotle**

C hallenging our beliefs is only the beginning. Once we dare to question what we've always accepted as truth, we have to go deeper. It's not just about what we've been believing, but why we've been believing it. And that's where self-reflection comes in.

I struggled for years to truly grasp the meaning of self-reflection. What it actually is and why it matters. For me, self-reflection is like pressing pause in the middle of the chaos or even the excitement of life. It's stepping back and asking myself, what's really going on here? Why am I feeling this way? Why am I responding this way? Why am I thinking this way?

Self-reflection isn't about getting lost in overthinking or replaying the past on an endless loop. I've done that more times than I care to admit, especially as someone who has carried a lot of self-doubt. But that's not what self-reflection is. It's not about staying stuck. It's about creating intentional space for clarity. It's about knowing yourself at a deeper level and uncovering truths that are hidden below the surface and asking yourself why they're there in the first place.

It's about aligning your thoughts, actions, and words with what genuinely matters to you. But first, you have to define what that is.

Self-reflection has been one of my most powerful tools for growth. It helped me recognize the patterns, emotions, and beliefs that shaped my choices, and the beliefs so deeply ingrained that I didn't even realize they were there until I stopped and looked.

For most of my life, I knew I wanted to be different. Not just different from my family or the way I was raised. Not running from my past. Just, different. I wanted to be someone who showed up in the world in a way that was loving, kind, and trustworthy. Someone who had the emotional intelligence to have meaningful conversations. Even the hard ones. Someone who could build deep relationships based on mutual trust, love, and understanding.

I knew I wanted a life that wasn't the life I had.

And while the roles that other people played in my life certainly influenced me, I had to take responsibility for how I was showing up in the world. That meant being intentional about self-reflection. Not just why it mattered, but understanding how to actually use it.

Self-reflection, for me, became a bridge. A bridge between who I was and who I was becoming. It wasn't about looking back just to dwell, or feel sorry for myself. It was about choosing, with intention, how I would move forward and become the best version of myself possible. It became a quiet but powerful declaration. I see myself. I honor where I've been. And now, I'm ready to grow and move forward.

At its core, self-reflection moved me from merely experiencing life to actually understanding it. It created a level of self-awareness that helped me examine not just what I was doing, but why. Why I spoke the way I did, reacted the way I did, and believed the things I did.

It also allowed me to assign meaning to the positive moments in my life. To see them, recognize them, and say I want more of that. It also gave me the ability to identify the areas where I needed to grow.

For those of us who have faced challenges, and honestly, that's most of us. Self-reflection isn't just useful. It's necessary.

It gives us a way to process our past. And for some, that past isn't just childhood or early adulthood. It might be last year. Last month. Yesterday. No matter the timeline, we all need a way to make sense of our difficult experiences, and even the mistakes we've made, so we can transform them into wisdom rather than baggage.

Through self-reflection, we are able to see the thought patterns, emotional triggers, and behaviors that shape our lives. Then we get to decide what we want to hold on to and what no longer serves us.

In many ways, self-reflection is the key to becoming more than who we are at this very moment. Without it, I know I risk operating on autopilot. Making choices based on old patterns, defaulting to what's easy, falling into past beliefs, and living under other people's expectations instead of my own values.

Without self-reflection, I might struggle to recognize my own mistakes, or worse, blame others more quickly than I should. I might even slip into a victim mentality without realizing it. And let me be clear. I was a victim. I experienced things that no one should have to endure. But I am not a victim anymore.

For a long time, I carried the weight of what happened to me. I let it shape my choices, my words, and my beliefs. Without realizing it, I was still operating from the place of who I had been rather than who I was now and who I was becoming.

And that's what self-reflection helped me see.

One of the clearest examples of this in my life was my relationship with my husband. In the early years of our marriage, whenever we disagreed or found ourselves in conflict, I would immediately feel attacked. Even if he was right. Even if what he was saying had merit. My walls went up, my defenses locked in, and suddenly, I wasn't just responding to my husband; I was reacting to my past.

I wasn't hearing him. I was hearing the echoes of every moment I had been dismissed, silenced, or made to feel like my words didn't matter.

And that realization was difficult to sit with.

I remember one argument in particular where something in his expression broke me. He looked hurt. Tired. Defeated. And I knew. I knew I wasn't fighting fair. I wasn't even fighting him. I was fighting every person before him who had ignored or dismissed me.

I stopped mid-sentence.

I took a breath.

And for the first time, I asked myself, What's really happening here?

The answers weren't easy. They unraveled years of wounds, patterns, and beliefs I didn't even know I was still carrying. But self-reflection gave me something I hadn't had before. A way forward. A way to separate my past from my present.

I started asking myself deeper questions. Not just in moments of conflict, but in my everyday life:

**Why do I feel this way?**

**What's really at the heart of my reaction?**

**How do I want to show up moving forward?**

At first, it felt awkward. I didn't know how to reflect in a way that felt productive. So I started small. I journaled. I let my thoughts spill onto the page without judgment. Simple questions like, What did I learn about myself today? Or What am I holding onto that no longer serves me? became my guideposts.

Over time, patterns emerged. I began to see how my past influenced my beliefs, my reactions, and the way I showed up in the world.

And I started making changes.

Meditation. Prayer. Sitting quietly, observing my thoughts, asking myself what do I want to change about how I respond to life?, all of it became part of my daily practice. These moments of stillness connected the dots between my thoughts, my actions, and my words.

Self-reflection is not just about what you discover. It's about what you do with those discoveries.

Each time I pause to reflect, I open the door to possibility.

I also give myself the chance to rethink my thoughts, evaluate my actions, and measure my words. Because of self-reflection, I am able to redefine how I will move forward. And if given the chance, it can do the same for you.

The more I practiced self-reflection, the more I saw myself. Not just who I had been, but who I was becoming. I started recognizing the ways my past shaped my choices, how I responded to life, and the patterns that held me back. But there was also something deeper that self-reflection uncovered.

It wasn't just about seeing myself more clearly. It was about what I saw when I looked.

I didn't always like what I found.

I could reflect on my choices, my beliefs, and my habits all day, but beneath it all, I had to face the truth. I didn't believe I was worthy. Not of love, not of success, not of taking up space, not of being more.

Self-reflection helped me see myself more clearly.

Self-worth taught me how to love what I saw.

# Chapter Nine

# Worthy Just As I Am

*"You yourself, as much as anybody in the entire universe, deserve your love and affection."*
— **Buddha**

Self-love and self-worth were foreign concepts to me. It wasn't something I was taught growing up, and it certainly wasn't something I saw modeled. Love, to me, was an outward act. Something I gave freely to others, even when they didn't deserve it. I knew how to pour myself out, how to meet the needs of those around me, and how to serve.

Even when my own cup was empty.

But loving myself? That was something else entirely.

I struggled with self-love because, deep down, I didn't believe I was worthy of it. I saw myself as someone who existed to prove my worth, to be useful, and to earn my place. But never to take up space for myself. And why would I?

I lacked confidence because I had spent years hearing that I would never amount to anything. That I wasn't good enough. That I was too much, too difficult, too loud, too messy. I was always causing trouble. I was stupid. I was nothing.

I heard it so often; I believed it.

That belief followed me into adulthood like a shadow I couldn't shake.

It showed up in the way I second-guessed myself. In the way I hesitated before speaking. In the way I made my self small when I should have taken up space. It showed up in my work where I had the skills, the experience, and the knowledge to hold my own against anyone. Yet, I convinced myself I didn't belong.

I constantly told myself I wasn't raised for this. I didn't have the right background, the polished words, the so-called pedigree.

Even when the leaders in the room turned to me to solve problems, bring ideas, and expand businesses, I doubted myself. I couldn't see that if I was propping others up, I could also stand on my own.

It showed up in motherhood, too. I didn't have a role model to look to, so I turned to books, to TV shows, to the mothers around me. And instead of trusting my instincts, I compared. I copied. I tried to fit into someone else's mold, only to feel like I was failing at every turn.

The same happened in my marriage. I floundered, trying to be the best partner I could be, and trying to figure out where the balance was between loving my husband and loving myself.

No matter where I turned, I felt like the world constantly shouted at me to be more, do more, prove more. And no matter how hard I tried, it never felt like enough. I never felt like enough.

So, I fell into a cycle of self-doubt, and endless comparison. Searching for external approval to fill a void that could only be mended from within.

## Breaking the Cycle

One day, I caught my reflection in the mirror, and this time, I didn't just see myself. I heard myself.

The words came so easily. So casually that I almost didn't notice them.

*"If only you were prettier."*
*"If only you were smarter."*
*"If only you were a better mom. A better wife. A better provider."*

And once the words started spilling out, they kept coming. Like an avalanche.

*"You'll never be enough."*
*"Push harder."*
*"Try harder."*

At this point in my life, if anyone else had dared to say those things to me, I wouldn't have tolerated it. I would have fought back, spoken up, drawn a line.

But when those words came from me?

They felt normal. They blended seamlessly into my day, looping like a broken record I had grown too used to hearing.

That day, standing in front of the mirror, something inside of me broke. Maybe it was clarity. Maybe it was exhaustion. Maybe I had finally had enough.

I heard the words I had spoken to myself and thought, I would never say that to anyone else.

And I realized I had to make a change.

I couldn't keep wounding myself with my own words. I couldn't keep rejecting myself. I needed to look around, take stock of how far I had come, and recognize that I was doing better than I gave myself credit for.

There was a little girl inside of me who had been hurt, overlooked, made to feel unworthy.

And she was counting on me.

No one was rooting for me harder than her.

She needed me to show up for her, to take her hand and say, I've got you now. You are safe. You are loved. You are enough. And, you are worth it. You are worth all of it.

## Unraveling the Lies

The words I spoke to myself weren't born from nowhere. They were echoes of a lifetime of lessons. Lessons that had taught me, long before I had the words to question them, that my worth was negotiable.

Those lessons started early.

My father's actions taught me that my value was something to be used and discarded. After my parents divorced, he moved away to be with a new partner, leaving me behind with relatives who didn't want me either. At a time when I needed love, guidance, and security, I found that I was mostly raising myself, clinging to scraps of worth wherever I could find them.

By the time I reached the summer before high school, I was desperate for something more. I saved every penny I could from odd jobs to buy schoolbooks, but I still lacked what I needed most. Support. Safety. Connection.

In my desperation, I called my mother, hoping to find a place of refuge. A home. I asked if I could come live with her.

Her answer was no.

She didn't have the space or the resources.

Her rejection wasn't just a refusal. It was confirmation of what I had feared for so long.

**I wasn't wanted. I wasn't enough. I wasn't worth the effort.**

With nowhere else to turn, I called my grandmother. She agreed to take me in, but her offer came with a chilling warning.

I should be prepared for "light petting and touching" from my grand-father.

Hearing those words as a teenager already yearning for safety and validation shattered me. In that moment, my worth felt like a bargaining chip in someone else's cruel game.

It took years to unlearn the lies I had absorbed about my value. Lies that told me I wasn't enough. Lies that whispered I was unworthy of love, safety, or belonging.

For a long time, I rationalized the choices of those who should have loved me the most. I told myself they had done the best they could, and that they had struggles of their own.

But as I grew older, I began to see the truth.

They had choices, just as I did.

And while it took me a while to choose differently, in the end, I have.

I couldn't control their choices, but I could control how I let those choices shape me moving forward.

## Learning To Love Myself

Realizing I needed to change the way I spoke to myself was one thing. Actually doing it? That was something else entirely.

At first, the idea of self-love felt forced. I had spent so many years believing I wasn't worthy of it. How was I supposed to suddenly start seeing myself differently?

So, like with everything else, I started small.

I paid attention to my inner dialogue. Every time I caught myself thinking you're not good enough or you don't belong, I paused and asked: Would I say that to someone I love? If the answer was no, I tried to soften the words.

I made space for self-kindness. On the days I felt exhausted or over-whelmed, instead of pushing harder, I asked: What do I need right now? Sometimes, the answer was rest. Other times, it was saying no without guilt.

I let myself celebrate small wins. For so long, I had dismissed my own successes, minimizing them as luck or circumstance. But I started acknowledging them, however small they were. You handled that conversation well. You showed up today. You're trying, and that matters.

I also practiced receiving love instead of deflecting it. When someone complimented me, instead of brushing it off, I let the words land. Thank you, I'd say, even when it felt uncomfortable.

Little by little, these small changes added up. They weren't grand gestures or sudden revelations. They were daily choices. Small but significant steps toward treating myself with the love and care I so readily gave to everyone else.

## Rewriting My Story

Self-love didn't come quickly or easily; it came in small, hesitant steps.

In the beginning, it felt foreign, even indulgent. But piece by piece, I began treating myself with the kindness I had longed for from others.

Self-love isn't a destination.

It's a daily choice. A commitment to treating yourself with the kindness you so freely give others.

And every time you choose it, you rewrite a piece of your story.

Now, I celebrate the fact that I keep going. Even when it's hard.

I see myself as worthy.

Not because I am perfect.

But because I am real.

The beautiful thing is that when you learn to love yourself, it doesn't just change you.

It changes how you show up in the world.

And once that happens, everything else begins to change.

Loving myself wasn't just about altering my inner dialogue or learning to treat myself with kindness. It was also about something deeper. Something harder. It was about choosing myself. Not just in quiet moments of self-reflection, but in the way I showed up for my own life.

Love isn't passive. It's not just words whispered in the dark or gentle affirmations spoken in front of a mirror. Love is action. Love is showing up.

I had spent years waiting for someone else to show up for me.

But as I began to see my self-worth, I also realized I had to show up for myself.

# Chapter Ten

# When I Realized I Had To Show Up For Myself

*"You can't go back and change the beginning, but you can start where you are and change the ending."*

**— C.S. Lewis**

I had to choose to be **fully engaged** in my own life. To go after the new life I wanted with intention. And I had to take responsibility for what was happening as a result of the new choices I was making.

That **life-changing magic,** showing up for myself in **bigger, wider, deeper ways than I ever had before,** required **trusting myself** and stepping forward in the direction I was choosing.

**For many years, survival was my only focus.** I wasn't living. I was bracing. I didn't have the luxury of slowing down to notice the little things. I was too busy preparing for the next storm, scanning my surroundings for danger, anticipating disappointment before it even had a chance to make itself known.

But beneath it all, I was also **waiting.**

Waiting for something to change.
Waiting to finally feel like I was enough.
Waiting to love myself enough.
Waiting for the past to loosen its grip on my heart and my mind.

And if I'm being completely honest, I also spent years waiting for someone else to fix things for me.

Even as I was on this journey of **rethinking, reclaiming, and taking ownership of who I was,** there was still a part of me looking for someone to **show me how to heal, how to put the pieces back together**. I wanted someone to see the parts of me I had hidden, the ones I was afraid to show others, and tell me I was still worthy.

Deep down, I think I wanted someone to **save me**.

But the reality was that **no one else could do that for me.**

Yes, I had people in my life who loved me. Yes, I had people who supported me along this journey. **But no one could show up for me in the way I needed to start showing up for myself.**

Not because they didn't love me.
Not because I wasn't worth loving.
But because **this was work only I could do.**

No one else could **advocate for my needs** the way I needed to.
No one else could **fight for me** harder than I was willing to fight for

myself.

No one else could **rewrite the old stories I had told myself** about my worth, my voice, or my place in the world.

No one else could **give me the life I craved. That was on me.**

## Choosing Myself on Purpose

Yes, I had been doing the hard work of **rewriting my narrative, unlearning toxic beliefs, changing my mindset, and learning to love myself,** but that was only part of the work.

I needed to go **deeper**.

I didn't wake up one morning with a **sudden, crystal-clear understanding** of exactly what that work entailed.

It was **slow**.
It was **messy**.
It was **a process of realization and acceptance.** Accepting a truth I had spent years avoiding.

**The only way my life was going to change, fully change, was if I changed it.**

I had to stop waiting to be rescued.
I had to start learning how to **rescue myself.**
How to **show up for myself.**
How to take **the growth, the healing, and the lessons I had experienced, and put them into action.**

I had to **choose myself on purpose.**

And that meant **showing up.**

Showing up for the exhausted, hurting version of myself who had been doing the best she could for years. Showing up for the woman I was becoming. Showing up for the life ahead of me. The one I had once been too afraid to believe in.

Because I deserved **more than just survival.**

I had to start making my needs **a priority instead of an afterthought**. I had to stop bending myself in half to accommodate everyone else while leaving **nothing for myself**. I had to stop **hoping that if I gave enough, loved enough, proved myself enough, then maybe I would finally feel like I mattered.**

I had to **stop abandoning myself.**

For years, I had mistaken **self-sacrifice for love**, as if giving until I had nothing left was proof of my worth.

**Real love includes loving yourself, too.**

It meant standing up for my needs, my well-being, and my voice. It meant **being on my own side.**

At first, I didn't know what showing up for myself **fully** looked like.

I just knew that it was something I **had to learn.**

It wasn't grand gestures or sweeping life changes. It wasn't waiting for the right moment.

It was **learning how to say no without apologizing.** It was **giving myself permission to rest without guilt.** It was **standing up for myself in conversations where I used to shrink.**

It was **reminding myself, over and over, that even if I failed, it was okay to get up and try again.**

Some days, it was as simple as **getting out of bed** when everything in me wanted to hide. Other days, it was **having the courage to ask for what I needed instead of assuming I had to handle everything alone.**

**Advocating for myself** meant acknowledging that **I mattered. Not because of what I could do for others, but because I was a person worthy of care, including my own.**

It was uncomfortable.
It felt unnatural.
And at times, it even felt **selfish.**

**But I kept going.**

**Self-abandonment had never saved me. It had only kept me small.** And I refused to live small any longer.

The more I showed up for myself, the more I realized:

I wasn't broken.
I wasn't unworthy.
I wasn't too far gone.

**I never was.**

The version of me I had been searching for, the one who felt safe and whole, **had been inside me all along.**

I just needed to **choose her.**

And once I did?

**There was no going back.**

# Chapter Eleven

# The Courage to Take Up Space

*"If you hear a voice within you say, 'You cannot paint,' then by all means paint, and that voice will be silenced."*

**— Vincent Van Gogh**

I f you want to talk about lacking confidence, **believe me, I could write the book.**

Oh wait. I am writing the book.

For years, I wore the crown. I was the queen of self-doubt. And I don't say that lightly. Today, self-doubt creeps in, and I have to work hard to guard against it. **Even after all the work I've done.**

The problem was, I didn't see myself as I was and as I could be.

I saw myself through the eyes of people who never thought I was good enough. **People who assigned me little to no value.** People who only cared about what they could take from me before tossing me aside.

Their judgments became my truth. Their voices became my inner dialogue.

And I believed them.

I believed I wasn't worth much. That I was just a shadow in the background. **Someone whose job was to serve, support, and stay small.**

Looking back now, I can see how **trapped** I was.

I spent years **confident in only one thing.** That I needed to prove my worth to other people.

I worked harder than anyone else. I showed up for everyone, even when I was exhausted, even when my own needs were buried beneath theirs.

I made myself **everything to everyone**, saying yes when my heart screamed no.

And I did it because I wanted so desperately to be **loved, accepted, and chosen.**

I thought shrinking myself was the only way to get there.

So I kept my voice soft. My opinions measured. My dreams locked away in a whisper.

Until sometimes, **I couldn't hold it in anymore.**

And when it finally bubbled up, **it didn't come out as strength or confidence. It came out as frustration, sharp words, or resentment I didn't know how to express.**

I had spent so much time swallowing my feelings, **contorting myself to fit the expectations of others**, that when my real voice finally pushed its way through, **it wasn't controlled. It wasn't graceful. It was messy, reactive, and sometimes even unfair.**

From the outside, I looked put together. Strong, capable, confident.

But inside?

**I was a mess of fear and loneliness.**

I was terrified of being *found out. A*s if someone would look too closely and discover that **I wasn't actually good enough after all.**

I perfected the art of self-loathing.

I picked myself apart with ease. I could rattle off a **laundry list** of every way I fell short.

Never smart enough. Never pretty enough. Never talented enough. Never **enough**.

And the irony?

**None of it was true.**

Even when I couldn't see my own worth, **I was out there building a life that defied my own limiting beliefs.**

I showed up as a mother. I**mperfect, yes, but determined.** I was committed to giving my children something **better, safer, and more stable than I had.**

And when I look at them today, **the way they love, the way they parent, the way they raise my grandchildren,** I know we changed something. We disrupted the generational trauma that had gone on for so long.

I showed up in my career, even when I doubted myself.

I remember driving past the headquarters of a major airline every day on my way to another job, telling myself:

**One day, I'm going to work there.**

Within a year, that statement became a reality.

Within a few months, I wasn't just working there. I was helping to write emergency response plans, leading trainings, and standing in front of rooms full of professionals who depended on me to guide them.

Me.

The girl who once believed she wasn't smart enough.

Later, I helped audit emergency plans for not one, but **two major cities,** knowing that my work would help people feel safer if disaster struck.

Then I moved into business. **Helping build six- and seven-figure companies for my husband and for other people.**

From the outside looking in, my life **seemed** full of confidence and power.

But the truth?

**I was still faking it.**

I pushed through my doubt. I plastered on a smile. **I showed up anyway.**

And for a long time, that was enough.

**Until it wasn't.**

## Confidence is Built. Not Given.

Loving myself changed **so much** for me.

But confidence? That was a different battle.

It didn't come all at once. It wasn't like flipping a switch. It came in awkward, uncertain steps.

Some days, I embraced it. Other days, I slipped back into my old ways of thinking.

But as I began to **fully embrace who I was, without apology, and without conditions, my confidence started to grow.**

And somewhere I learned that confidence isn't about being perfect. It isn't about never feeling doubt or fear.

Confidence is built on the quiet belief that you are worthy. And because you are worthy, you show up.

I am worthy.

**Worthy of success.**
**Worthy of love.**

**Worthy of happiness.**
**Worthy of belonging.**

And that worthiness isn't tied to how much we accomplish.

It isn't even about how others see us.

**It's about how much we trust ourselves.**

**Confidence is self-trust.**

It's believing you will show up, you will try, you will take the next step, **even when you're scared.**

For years, I thought confidence was something other people were born with. Like a personality trait that I simply didn't have.

But I was wrong.

Confidence is something you build.

It's a muscle that grows stronger every time you stand up for yourself. Every time you step outside your comfort zone. Even if you fail.

Even if it doesn't go as planned.

The real power is in showing up.

Even when you don't succeed every time.

## Your Turn

If you're reading this and struggling with confidence, you need to know that you are not alone.

I know what it feels like to doubt yourself so deeply that you're afraid to even try.

But confidence doesn't come from waiting until you feel ready.

It comes from showing up, anyway.

If I had waited until I felt ready, I wouldn't be here writing this book.

I wouldn't have built a life that defied the voices in my head.

I wouldn't have become the woman I am today.

So start small. Celebrate the wins. Even the little ones.

Show up for yourself the way you show up for everyone else.

Speak kindly to yourself. Even when it feels strange.

And most importantly?

Love yourself first.

Because confidence, at its core, is simply self-love in motion.

It's already inside of you.

You just have to believe it.

So let me ask you,

What would happen if you stopped waiting for confidence and just started showing up?

# Chapter Twelve

---

# Reclaiming Yourself from Your Past

"You are not meant to become a different person. You are meant to
return to yourself."

— **Nayyirah Waheed**

If finding my voice was the beginning, reclaiming the parts I had
hidden was the next step.

After all the effort it took to take up space, to stop shrinking,and to
speak my truth, another challenge emerged. One I hadn't expected. I
had to go back. Not to relive the past, but to retrieve the parts of me
I'd left behind along the way.

The parts I'd buried.
The parts I was told to be ashamed of.
The parts that felt too broken, too loud, too soft, too much.

I spent so much of my life trying to outrun the past. To push it away.
To pretend it didn't shape me.

We're told to "move on" and "let it go," as if pain has an expiration
date. As if healing is a straight line.

That's cute advice.
It's also kind of bullshit.

Because our past isn't always something to escape.
Sometimes, it holds the very pieces we need to move forward.

## What We Carry

For years, I thought if I ignored my past, it would lose its power.
But it didn't.

It was there in the choices I made.
In the relationships I clung to, or in the ones that I avoided.
In the way I talked to myself when no one else could hear.

Every triumph. Every misstep. Every wound.
It all shaped how I showed up in the world.

Not just as a woman.
As a mother.
As a friend.
As a leader.

The challenge wasn't to erase my past. It was to own it in a way that served me. To separate the lessons from the limitations.
To stop carrying stories that were never mine to begin with.

And that required work.

Hard, vulnerable, honest work.

I had to seek support.
I had to face what I had avoided.
I had to forgive others, and I had to forgive myself.

## Rewriting the Meaning

There were seasons where the weight of my past felt unbearable.

I didn't know how to move forward while dragging so much shame, regret, and grief behind me.

But slowly, I began to redefine what my story meant.

Not by pretending it was all okay.
Not by painting it prettier than it was.

But by choosing what I carried forward, and what I left behind.

My past no longer defined me. It informed me. And that distinction was life changing.

When I looked at my past through the lens of shame, all I could see were mistakes.

But when I looked through the lens of grace? I saw strength. I saw resilience. I saw a woman who kept showing up, even when it hurt.

And that? **That's power.**

## Forgiveness Is Freedom

One of the hardest parts of reclaiming my story was forgiving myself.

I had made choices I wasn't proud of.
Some born from survival.
Some from fear.
Some from not knowing any better at the time.

And I carried guilt for too long.

Guilt for what I didn't know.
Guilt for who I wasn't ready to be.
Guilt for taking so long to become the woman I am now.

But that guilt didn't make me better.
It just kept me stuck.

So I let it go. Not because I didn't care, but because I finally did.

I forgave the younger version of me who didn't have the tools.
Who did the best she could with what she had.
Who was trying to protect herself, even when it didn't look like it.

And in doing that, I made space for a new story to emerge.

I no longer have to pretend that my past doesn't exist. And neither do you.
You don't have to carry it like a weight either.

You get to choose what it means now, and into the future.
You get to choose what comes with you, and what doesn't.

So let me ask you:

- What part of your story have you been running from?

- What would change if you stopped seeing it as a failure, and started seeing it as a foundation?

- What do you need to reclaim so that you can redefine your life?

Because reclaiming your past isn't about living there.
It's about returning to yourself.

The whole you.
The beautiful, messy, complicated truth of you.
The one who survived.
The one who's still standing.
The one who's just getting started.

You are not what happened to you.

You are what you choose to do with it.

# Chapter Thirteen

# Still I Rise: On Strength, Resilience, and Reclaiming Joy

*"The wound is the place where the Light enters you."*

**— Rumi**

### Inner Strength

One of the most important skills I've had to develop is inner strength. I call it a skill because that's exactly what it is. Something that only grows through practice, through resistance, through repetition. In the beginning, I believed mine was weak. Maybe it wasn't. Maybe that strength had been there all along, buried beneath the noise of doubt and survival. Still, I had to dismantle the version of strength I had been taught. One built on appearances and silence, and I had to rebuild it into something real.

Something that could carry me forward.

Inner strength didn't just appear one day. It wasn't something I stumbled upon by accident or something I was lucky enough to be born with. It's not an exclusive trait reserved for a select few. **Inner strength is built. It's cultivated. It's a quiet force that grows stronger every time you decide to stand up, move forward, or simply hold on when everything inside you wants to let go.**

If you had asked me 20 years ago what inner strength was, I wouldn't have known how to define it. Back then, I thought strength meant never falling apart, never showing weakness, and never asking for help. I thought strength had to be loud, visible, and something people could admire from the outside. I thought that even though I was quiet and often faded into the background; I had to project an image of strength, one that looked unshakable. Because that's what I had been taught to believe.

But over time, life taught me a different lesson. I began to understand that true strength isn't always visible. **And it doesn't always roar.**

Most of the time, inner strength is quiet. It's the moment you decide to keep going when you want to give up. It's the courage to take small steps forward when the path is uncertain. It's trusting yourself to rise again, even when getting back up takes longer than you expected.

For me, inner strength didn't arrive in a single moment. It was something I discovered along the way, in the hardest, darkest moments of my life.

I was so young when I had my first daughter. Too young. Barely an adult myself, and suddenly, I had this tiny life in my arms depending on me for everything. I had no idea how I was going to take care of her. My family, in all the ways that mattered, had abandoned me. I was alone. I was scared. I was vulnerable. I was broken.

And I had nowhere to go.

One night, as I held my little girl in my arms and thought about the future, I wasn't sitting in a beautifully decorated nursery. I wasn't in the front room of a safe, warm home.

I was sitting in my car.

That's all we had.

The weight of it hit me so hard I could barely breathe. I remember looking down at her tiny, perfect face and feeling this crushing wave of fear.

**How did we get here?**
**How was I going to protect her?**
**How was I going to do this?**

The tears came hot and fast. I cried because I didn't have the answers. I cried because I had never felt so hopeless and alone.

And yet, somewhere in the middle of that fear, something inside me stirred.

I looked at her peaceful little face, the way she trusted me completely, and I knew. **I would do whatever it took to give her the life she deserved.**

In that moment I discovered A quiet fire. A strength I didn't know I had.

That small glimmer of hope became my steady ground. I moved from despair to determination. I reached down deep inside myself and found something I hadn't known was there. I didn't have a plan. I didn't have support. But I had a reason to keep going. And for me, that was enough.

Inner strength didn't erase my pain. It didn't make my obstacles disappear. It didn't mean I wasn't afraid or uncertain or overwhelmed by the enormity of my situation.

But it gave me the courage to take the next step. And the next. And the next.

Raising my daughter while working, going to school, and trying to survive wasn't easy. There were weeks when my paycheck barely covered rent and food. Times when I had to choose between diapers for my daughter or food for myself. **She always won.** She was always my first choice.

There were nights when doubt crept in, whispering that I wasn't strong enough, that I wasn't good enough. That even though I was giving it my all, it still might not be enough.

**The voices of doubt were loud.**

And I wanted to quit.

Not quit her. Never her.

But quit the fight. Because I felt like I was failing.

Inner strength didn't show up all at once. It was something I had to build. One choice at a time.

Every time I decided to keep going, even when I didn't want to or didn't think I could, my strength grew. Every small victory. Like paying rent on time, seeing my daughter laugh, buying her a toy, finishing a project at work, watching her smile, became proof that I could do hard things.

And those moments taught me to trust myself, even when my world felt shaky.

For me, inner strength is a lot like the roots of a tree.

It keeps me grounded when life gets hard.

It doesn't mean I won't bend. It doesn't mean I won't lose a few leaves.

But it does mean that when the storms come, I won't break.

And every storm you survive causes your roots to grow deeper. Stronger. More unshakable.

So if you're reading this and wondering if you have inner strength, let me assure you, you do. It's already there. Inside of you.

You might not feel it right now. It might be buried under layers of doubt, fear, or pain.

But I promise you, it's there.

And you've probably already proven it in ways you don't even realize.

Think back to a time when you kept going, even when it was hard.

A time when you stood up for yourself or someone else.

A time when you didn't give up, even when everything inside you wanted to.

That's inner strength.

My little girl is now a mom herself. She's in her 30s.

**We made it.**

I kept going. I created my life. I built a career. I raised her and her siblings.

And through it all, inner strength gave me the ability to move beyond where I was. To not give up, to keep going.

What helped me? Hunger for more. A belief that things could get better. A belief not just in myself, but in my ability to create change.

Whatever that hope is for you, that belief, that fire inside you, that's where your inner strength lives.

It's in the choices you make every day. To keep showing up. To keep fighting for yourself and the people you love.

Inner strength isn't about never failing. I failed many times.

Inner strength is about trusting yourself to rebuild.

It's not about having all the answers. It's about having the courage to take the first step forward.

It's the voice inside you that says:

**I can do this.**

**I will rise again.**

And, you will rise again.

You have the strength to handle whatever is in front of you.

**What's one small step you can take today to honor your inner strength?**

Maybe it's getting out of bed.

Maybe it's saying no to something that drains you.

Maybe it's saying yes to something that scares you.

Maybe it's simply reminding yourself that you are strong, capable, and worthy of a life that feels good to live.

Because you are.

**And every time you lean into that quiet, unshakable force inside you, it grows.**

Inner strength is your foundation.

**Trust it. Build on it.**

And watch what happens next.

## Resilience

Once I began to understand what inner strength truly was, I started drawing on it more and more. And as I did, something else developed alongside it. Another force that walked hand in hand with my strength.

That force was **resilience**.

If inner strength is what held me steady, resilience is what helped me rise. It's what taught me to adapt, to move forward, to move smarter, faster, wiser, and stronger. To keep going no matter what life threw my way.

Resilience also didn't mean I never fell apart. I did. Many times.

There were moments when life knocked me flat, when I struggled to get back up, when the weight of it all made me wonder if I could take one more step. And that was okay.

The pain was real. The setbacks were real. The tears were real.

And they mattered.

They shaped me. They lit a fire inside me. A fire that refused to be extinguished.

There were moments when I sat in the weight of it all, grieving what had been lost, what I was losing, what I was still fighting through. Some days, resilience meant allowing myself to feel, to sit with the pain, to cry, and to acknowledge the sheer exhaustion of it all.

But after I allowed myself that space, I had to get up, wash my face, and fix my mascara. Then I had to get about the business of overcoming.

Resilience isn't about never struggling. It's about knowing that even when life sets you back, it doesn't have to keep you there.

It taught me to shift my thinking from Why me? To what's next?

It helped me refuse to let hardship write my story for me. Instead, I began picking up the pen and writing the next chapter myself.

I had been a victim of my circumstances. That was true. But I didn't have to stay one.

And resilience was what helped me break free.

It helped me release the past and claim something new.

A new story.

A new life.

A new belief in myself.

**I am strong.**
**I am capable.**
**I am brave enough to rise**and **rise again.**


## Resilience is built. Not Born.

Resilience wasn't something I was born with.

It was something I had to build. Piece by piece, alongside inner strength.

I had to learn how to persevere through life's hardest lessons.

And I wish I could say those lessons came gently.

But they didn't.

More often than not, they came when I was pushed to my limits. When I was forced to face moments that left me questioning everything.

One of those moments came when I was just a child.

## The Day That Changed Me

The doorbell rang, shattering the silence of the house like a gunshot.

I huddled on the cold bathroom floor, my small hands trembling, and my heart pounding in my chest.

My mother lay beside me. Lifeless, unmoving, lost in a battle with demons that had taken on my father's face.

This was the second time I had watched her try to escape the abuse that had become our family's twisted norm.

I was only seven or eight years old, but I understood one thing with absolute clarity;

Something was terribly wrong.

Fear thickened the air, pressing down on me.

In a panic, I gathered the pills scattered across the tile, my small fingers fumbling as I tried to flush them away, desperate to erase the evidence of her suffering.

The doorbell rang again. And again. And again.

Whoever was outside wasn't leaving.

I took a deep breath, trying to steady myself. My mother was unresponsive on the floor, and someone, someone angry and impatient, was pounding at the door.

I stood up on shaking legs, forcing myself to move. When I opened the door, I found myself staring up at a man I recognized, the pastor from our small-town church.

I had seen him before, standing at community gatherings, speaking gentle words over fried fish at the local church dinners.

But today, there was no gentleness.

His eyes were hard.

His voice was sharp.

And his anger sent chills down my spine.

*"I need to see your mother. Right now."*

My voice, small and trembling, barely made it out.

*"She can't come to the door."*

I waited for a moment of kindness. A flicker of compassion for a child standing in the middle of so much chaos.

But instead, his expression darkened. His jaw clenched. His eyes narrowed.

*"Your low-life, good-for-nothing father has run off with my little girl,"* he barked. *"Your mother better help me get her back."*

His words hit me like a slap.

Shock coursed through me. But deep down, I wasn't surprised.

My father had always had a penchant for pretty girls. And even at my young age, I understood what the pastor meant.

My father and his daughter, barely eighteen, had vanished together.

And now, I was standing in the doorway, caught between two nightmares.

Behind me, my mother lay on the floor, unconscious.

In front of me, an enraged man demanded answers.

And in that moment, a lesson was born.

A lesson that would help shape the foundation of my future.

## The Lessons Resilience Taught Me

Life has a way of throwing immense challenges our way, often when we least expect them.

And while those challenges can leave scars, they also offer something else;

An invitation to rise.

Standing in that doorway, I began to understand, even if I couldn't put words to it yet, that resilience isn't about never feeling pain.

It's about finding the strength to move forward despite it.

In the years that followed, I would look back on that day.

The day I stood at the threshold of chaos and confusion.

And I would realize something powerful.

Every struggle holds a lesson.

That moment taught me how to stand in the face of fear.

How to make choices even when none seemed right.

How to keep moving forward when the weight of the world tried to hold me down.

Each experience, no matter how painful, helped me forge resilience alongside strength.

I could write a trilogy on my hardships. My failures.

There were moments when I felt like giving up.

Moments when I questioned whether I was capable of overcoming.

But now, I know the truth.

Resilience is not about avoiding hardship.

It's about learning to rise, because of it and in spite of it.

Every setback holds a lesson if we're willing to look for it.

And when I started **pairing resilience with inner strength,** something wonderful happened.

I realized that one helped me stand. The other helped me move.

And suddenly, every difficulty, every failure, every moment of doubt?

They became stepping stones.

## Inner Strength and Resilience Clear the Way for Joy

For years, it looked like I was happy on the outside. But deep down?

I struggled to connect with true joy.

I carried so much pain. So much fear. So much self-doubt.

Joy felt impossible to hold on to.

But when I learned to rise above my challenges, to embrace the lessons within them, and let go of the weight that held me down, my joy came back.

Joy doesn't require a perfect life.

It requires a brave heart.

A heart willing to see beauty, even in the mess.

Resilience and strength were shaping something new inside me.

They were making space for joy to live.

And if you let them, they'll do the same for you.

## Finding Joy

When I first began to comprehend the depth of inner strength, it felt like finding solid ground after years of drifting. That strength kept me steady when life's storms raged, but it didn't shield me from every hit. Resilience taught me how to rise, how to stand after falling, how to adapt, and how to keep moving forward, even when the weight of life threatened to pull me under.

And yet, something was still missing.

For a long time, I thought resilience was the final piece. The key to navigating life's challenges. If I could just be strong enough, if I could keep rising no matter how many times I fell, then maybe, just maybe, I'd be okay.

But as I leaned into my inner strength and embraced resilience, I began to realize there was something else quietly waiting for me.

Something softer. Something lighter.

Something that could make all the struggle feel worth it.

That something was joy.

## Joy Didn't Erase the Hardships. It Transformed Them.

Tapping into joy didn't mean my hardships had disappeared. The bills still came. The losses still stung. The struggles still knocked me flat some days.

Choosing joy didn't change my circumstances.

But it changed how I moved through them.

It gave my journey more meaning. It became a light to hold onto when the darkness felt overwhelming.

Joy didn't erase my pain, but it softened its edges.

It reminded me that I wasn't just surviving. I was living.

## Joy is a Choice

It took me years to understand that joy isn't something that just happens to you.

It's something you choose.

A deliberate, sometimes difficult choice.

At every moment, I had a decision to make. Surrender to my hardships and let them consume me, or look up, take a breath, and choose to see the good, even if I had to search for it.

Not just in the world around me, but in myself.

That wasn't an easy lesson to learn.

Growing up, joy wasn't something I saw often. Not in the world. And certainly not in the mirror.

I used to believe that joy was something big. Something reserved for those movie-like moments where everything falls into place. Where the music swells, and suddenly, life is perfect.

That's what I thought for so long.

I was wrong.

Joy doesn't need a grand stage.

It doesn't shout. More often, it whispers.

It hides in the ordinary, and in the moments we so often overlook.

It's in the sound of a child's laughter. So full and free that it feels like music.

It's in the warmth of the sun on your skin on a crisp morning.

It's in the way a friend squeezes your hand at just the right moment.

It's in the kindness of a stranger's smile, the bloom of a flower pushing through cracked pavement, the soft press of a baby's kiss on your cheek.

Joy isn't always loud.

But it's there.

You just have to look for it.

## Joy Doesn't Ignore the Pain. It Makes Space for Something More

Choosing joy doesn't mean ignoring the hard things.

The grief, the disappointments, the struggles, they're still part of me.

They still demand my attention sometimes.

But I've learned I don't have to give them all of me.

Choosing joy means making room for something else to exist alongside the pain.

It's like opening a window in a stifling room, and letting in light and fresh air, even while the mess still covers the floor.

The struggle is real.

But so is the beauty.

## Joy, Strength and Resilience Feed Each Other

The beautiful thing is that joy, strength and resilience aren't separate.

They fuel each other.

Joy strengthens you from the inside out.

It fuels your resilience and your strength.

It gives you the courage and energy to rise one more time, even when you feel like you can't.

And strength and resilience, in turn, create the space for joy to take root and grow.

I've learned that joy doesn't demand perfection.

It doesn't wait for life to be easy.

It shows up in the mess. In the struggle.

In the moments when you think you can't take one more step.

Joy is what transforms mere survival into living.

**Strength. Resilience. Joy.**

Together, they form the foundation of a life, not free from struggle, but one that rises above it.

They remind us that we don't have to choose between the hard and the beautiful.

We can hold both.

The pain and the possibility.

The weight of the past and the hope of the future.

The scars and the healing.

The tears and the laughter.

Joy is still here.

Waiting for you to notice it.

Where Can You Choose Joy Today?

Where can you lean into your strength today?

Where can you let resilience carry you?

And most importantly, what small moment of joy can you choose to see?

Because I promise you, it's there.

Waiting quietly.

Waiting patiently.

Waiting for you.

You've come so far.

And you are not finished yet.

Step forward.

It's time to rise.

# Chapter Fourteen

# The Life in Front of You

*"Tell me, what is it you plan to do with your one wild and precious life?"*
— **Mary Oliver**

### The Power of Presence

My journey to disrupt my default is ongoing, and it's unfolding in its own imperfect rhythm. It's messy, winding, and marked by peaks that lift me high and valleys that pull me back down. Some days, I feel unstoppable, fully aligned with the life I want to create. Other days, the weight feels heavier. I stumble. Progress feels elusive, like taking two steps forward only to slide three steps back.

The difference between who I was then and who I am now lies in my persistence. I keep going. I don't stop. I don't give up. I've learned to pause, evaluate where I am, and make the adjustments needed to bring me closer to where I want to be. I've discovered that growth isn't about perfection. It's about showing up for myself time and time again, even when it's hard. I strive to live intentionally, creating the life I want to live, rather than simply coasting along to keep the peace like I once did.

And one of the most important things I've learned on this journey is the ability to simply be.

Not just exist. I spent too many years doing that. Rushing through my days, holding my breath until the next thing. I mean the art of *truly being*. Being present. Being aware. Being alive in the moment instead of racing past it to something else.

Life is busy. Loud. A relentless to-do list that never seems to shrink. There's always another task, another worry, another regret replaying in the back of my mind like a movie I didn't even like the first time. Always planning, fixing, thinking ahead, or looking back. It's exhausting.

For so long, I was so caught up in staying busy that I didn't realize how much I was missing. I spent days, years even, lost in my own noise and fixated on what I couldn't change or anxious about what might come next. The present moment slipped through my fingers again and again, traded for worry, regret, and distraction. Moments I can never reclaim.

Over time, I've come to understand that the present moment is where life truly happens. It's where the good stuff is. Reflecting on the past has its place. It teaches us. It grounds us. And it reminds us how far we've come. Looking ahead is important, too. It helps us plan, dream, and grow. Both matter. But we can't *live* in either. The living? That happens here, in the *now*.

At the time of writing this book, my husband and I have been married for 25 years. When we walked into this marriage, we brought more than just love. We carried baggage. Heavy bags packed with past hurts, unspoken fears, unresolved trauma, lofty expectations, and fragile dreams. And in those early years, we let that baggage dictate far too much.

We spent countless hours living in the past. Revisiting old wounds, and trying to rewrite moments we couldn't change. At the same time, we were consumed by fear of the future. We spent too much of our time spinning through endless "what ifs" as if imagining them could somehow prepare us. We were busy, always busy, but not fully alive. We weren't present. Not in the life we were trying to build, and certainly not with each other.

My husband, the strong and steady cowboy type, is a man of few words. He doesn't speak just to fill the silence; when he speaks, it's because he has something worth saying. And one day, in the midst of a particularly chaotic season, a day where the stress was thick, the complaints relentless, and the air between us heavy, he broke through the noise.

I was caught in a storm of frustration, trying to hold everything together while feeling like I was unraveling. I barely noticed him step toward me until he gently hugged me. His grip was firm but comforting, a tether pulling me back to the moment. He looked at me with the quiet intensity I've come to rely on and said, "Take a breath. We're going to be okay. This isn't danger. It's just stress."

His words weren't eloquent or poetic. They were simple. Direct. Exactly what I needed. He didn't try to fix me or dismiss my feelings. Instead, he invited me to pause. To breathe.

That moment didn't fix everything. The stress didn't evaporate, and the challenges of our life together didn't disappear. But in that brief pause, we found something rare and precious: presence. We noticed, not the stress, not the frustration, but each other. The warmth. The quiet. The here and now.

That pause taught me something I've carried with me ever since: the power of noticing. Of being fully present. Of choosing to stay connected to the moment, even in the mess.

I didn't know it then, but there's a name for that kind of awareness. It's called mindfulness.

Not the buzzword kind. Not the overly polished, cross-legged-on-a-mountain kind. I'm talking about the kind that meets you in your real life.

Mindfulness isn't about erasing the chaos. It's not about shutting down your thoughts or achieving some impossible state of perfect calm. It's about noticing. It's about choosing to see what's real, what's here, and what's now, even in the middle of life's messiness.

At first glance, it doesn't always seem practical. In the rush of everyday life, with all its demands and distractions, the idea of slowing down to notice something as simple as sunlight on your skin might feel out of reach, or even indulgent. Yet, that's exactly where its power lies.

Mindfulness is the practice of tuning into the present moment, no matter how ordinary or chaotic it might be. It's noticing the gentle warmth of the sun on your face or the sound of laughter spilling from the next room. It's feeling your breath as it moves in and out of your body, a steady rhythm that anchors you to right now.

It's not about fixing yourself or silencing your thoughts. It's about allowing yourself to fully experience what you're feeling, without judgment, and without trying to change it. It's simply being present with whatever is happening in this moment, and giving yourself the grace to just be.

It's also a practice. One that takes time and intention. Our minds love to race ahead, to worry, to plan, to fix. Mindfulness is the gentle act of bringing yourself back. Back to this breath, this moment, this life. It doesn't make the chaos disappear, but it quiets the overwhelm. It offers space to breathe, to think, to reconnect with what truly matters.

I won't pretend it's always easy. My mind still wanders. Old habits of overthinking still creep in. But every time I choose to pause, every time I choose to simply be, I remind myself that the present moment is a gift. It's where life happens. It's where love grows. It's where healing begins.

Mindfulness taught me to stop missing my life. To stop running on autopilot and start paying attention. It gave me back the moments I used to overlook. The small but powerful moments of joy, clarity, and connection that make life worth living.

When was the last time you paused? Truly paused? Not to scroll your phone, or solve a problem, or plan for tomorrow. But to simply breathe. To feel. To notice the life you're in right now?

The good stuff isn't somewhere far off in the future or hidden in the past. It's here. Waiting for you to see it.

## Gratitude

Even as I began to rethink, reclaim, and redefine my life, there were still days when it all felt like too much. Let's be real. Life didn't magically get easier just because I started learning to love myself or practicing mindfulness.

The demands didn't slow down. The pressures didn't disappear. I was running a business, raising my children, helping with homework, and managing a house that always felt one mess away from chaos. I was juggling it all, and if I'm honest, I wasn't doing it very gracefully.

Most days, I felt like I was barely keeping my head above water, grasping for something. Anything that could steady me.

It was in the middle of this loud, chaotic, beautiful mess that I stumbled into gratitude. And I do mean stumbled. I didn't arrive at it full of wisdom or enlightenment; I came to it because I was desperate. Something had to change.

At first, I wasn't convinced. Gratitude sounded nice in theory, but it also sounded a little... fluffy. I remember thinking, *What good will writing down a list of things I'm thankful for do when I'm exhausted and overwhelmed?* But desperation has a way of making you try things you wouldn't normally consider, so I gave it a shot.

I started small. Really small.

On one of those long, heavy days, I sat down and forced myself to write three things I could appreciate in that moment. My first list wasn't profound:

1. The smell of my morning coffee.

2. My children's giggles echoing down the hallway.

3. The way a stranger smiled and held the door for me at the store.

That's it. Nothing groundbreaking. Yet, as I looked at those three simple things, something shifted. It wasn't dramatic. Just a thread of calm weaving itself through the chaos. For a moment, I wasn't drowning in everything that felt overwhelming. I wasn't stuck replaying all the ways I was "falling short" or worrying about what was next. I was just here, holding onto these small, good things that might've otherwise gone unnoticed.

So I did it again. And again. Day by day, I started noticing more. The way the trees were beginning to bloom in the backyard. The comfort of my favorite sweatshirt, still warm from the dryer. The satisfaction of finally crawling into bed after a long, exhausting day.

These tiny moments began to pile up, and I realized what was happening.

I was shifting my focus.

Gratitude didn't erase the hard stuff. It didn't make my challenges disappear or suddenly make life easy. But it softened the edges of my struggle and gave me a place to rest.

I remember one season in particular when life felt especially heavy. My mother was battling ovarian cancer, and I was deep in the trenches of caregiving, and trying to be strong for her while juggling everything else; work, family, my own emotions. It was difficult.

It felt impossible to balance.

One day, I sat beside her in a quiet moment. Her hand was in mine, and I remember noticing the warmth of her skin.

It struck me, this simple thing. Her warmth.

Growing up, warmth wasn't something I felt from her very often. Our relationship had always been complicated, marked by distance and unmet needs. Yet in that moment, I felt it. Her hand in mine, soft and steady. It brought me comfort in a way I hadn't experienced before.

I could have overlooked it. I could have let the hopelessness and grief of the situation consume me. But instead, I held onto that moment. I allowed myself to feel gratitude. Not just for her warmth, but for the chance to be there with her, and to share that fleeting connection.

As I looked around, I began to see other small things to hold on to. The sound of birds outside her window and the way sunlight filtered through the blinds and painted the room in gold. None of these moments changed our reality.

My mother was still sick and dying. I was still exhausted.

But these tiny sparks of goodness grounded me.

Gratitude, I realized, isn't about ignoring pain or pretending everything is fine. It's about seeing what's still good, even when life feels unbearably hard. It's about noticing the beauty that exists right alongside the mess.

As I continued practicing gratitude, it became more than just a list, it became a way of seeing the world. I stopped focusing so much on what was missing and started paying attention to what was already there. Gratitude didn't solve all my problems, but it gave me perspective. It reminded me that even when life felt overwhelming, there was always something worth noticing.

If you're feeling overwhelmed or stuck, I want you to know that I get it. I've been there. Gratitude doesn't have to be grand or complicated. Start small. Write down one thing, then another. Let it guide your focus, little by little.

Gratitude won't erase your struggles, but it will shift how you see them. It will help you look closer, to find the light even in the darkest moments. And when you do, you'll discover that gratitude doesn't just change your perspective, it changes you.

Gratitude gave me a sense of wholeness I didn't know I was missing. It steadied me during life's hardest seasons and softened me in ways I never expected.

Most importantly, it taught me that no matter how hard life gets, there's always something to be thankful for.

Always something worth noticing.

What's one small thing you can appreciate right now? Pause. Look around. It's there, waiting for you to see it.

## Reflection

The truth is, my journey to live fully and intentionally is still un-folding. It's full of twists and turns, hard-earned lessons, and days that stretch me more than I'd like to admit. Some days, I feel deeply grounded, as though I'm standing on steady ground, fully present and grateful for the life I'm building. Other days, I lose my footing. Old habits resurface, and the weight of everything I'm juggling pulls me back into autopilot.

What's changed isn't that I've figured it all out or that I never stumble. It's that I've learned to keep showing up. Even on the hard days, I choose to return to the moment.

To notice. To appreciate. To keep moving forward, one small step at a time.

For years, I told myself that life would begin "someday" once every-thing fell into place, once I felt ready, once the hard seasons were behind me.

I believed the good stuff lived somewhere in the future, waiting for me to arrive. What I didn't realize is that life doesn't wait. It's happening right now, even in the middle of the mess. The moments we think of as too small, too ordinary, or too fleeting.

They're the ones that make up our lives.

Learning to be present taught me to pause. Practicing gratitude taught me to see what I once overlooked. Together, they changed how I move through life. Less fixing, more being.

The life I want to create? It doesn't exist somewhere off in the distance.

It begins *here*.

With this moment.
This breath.
This choice to *pay attention*.

And that changes *everything*.

*Reclaiming who you are is only the beginning. Now, the question is: What will you do with this life you've claimed?*

# Part 3

---

Redefine – Creating What Comes Next

Shadow Scribe Media

# Chapter Fifteen

---

# The Courage To Be Clear

*"You don't have a right to the cards you believe you should have been dealt. But you have an obligation to play the hell out of the ones you're holding."*
— **Cheryl Strayed**

C hange is hard. Communicating that change out loud? Even harder.

When you start redefining your life, shifting old patterns, and stepping into a stronger version of yourself, something inevitable happens: the people around you will notice. Some will celebrate your growth. Others may resist it. And in those moments when the expectations people once had of you no longer fit who you're becoming, you'll face a critical challenge. The courage to be clear.

For me, that challenge began with boundaries.

At one point in my life, I had no clue what it meant to set healthy boundaries. I didn't know what they looked like, how to create them, or, honestly, if I was even allowed to have them. Growing up and well into my early adulthood, every boundary that should have been a fundamental right; my right as a woman, as a human being, was ignored, trampled over, or dismissed as unimportant.

The message I internalized was clear.
My needs didn't matter.
My time didn't matter.
My safety didn't matter.
I didn't matter.

And so I gave and gave. My energy, my time, my body, and my voice. I gave so much of myself away that for a long time, there wasn't much left to hold on to. I became someone I didn't recognize. Someone exhausted, resentful, and quietly aching for the very love and respect I wasn't giving to myself.

For people like me, people who have endured the trauma of abuse, neglect, or abandonment, boundaries can feel impossible. When your heart has spent years starving for love, affection, and acceptance, it's easy to convince yourself that you have to compromise to obtain it. That you have to say "yes" to everything, even when you mean "no." That you have to accept the unacceptable just to feel wanted.

I had to learn the hard truth. Love that demands you betray yourself isn't love at all.

It took me years to understand this. Boundaries aren't selfish. They're not cruel. They're not a punishment you place on others. Setting boundaries is an act of love. Love for yourself and love for the people in your life. It's not just a right. It's essential.

Boundaries are the framework that protects what matters most. Your time, energy, body, heart, mind, and the health of your relationships.

At first, this realization felt impossible to live out. I thought boundaries were walls. Cold, hard barriers that would shut people out or hurt their feelings. But I was wrong.

Boundaries, I came to realize, are like the nervous system of your life. They alert you when something is off, help you respond with intention, and keep everything functioning in balance. They're not walls. They're wisdom in motion.

And then I learned something else. Something even more profound. Boundaries aren't just about saying "no." They're also about giving what I call a *clean yes*.

A clean yes is when you say "yes" because you genuinely mean it. Not because you feel pressured, obligated, or afraid of disappointing someone. It's a yes that feels light, honest, and free of resentment.

Let me tell you, this shift in thinking was life-changing for me. For so long, I had said yes out of guilt or fear. Fear of losing love. Fear of rejection. Fear of being left behind. But every dishonest yes, every yes that came with a grudge, a clenched jaw, or a quiet ache, was a tiny betrayal of me. And over time, those little betrayals added up.

I had to let go of the belief that saying "no" made me unlovable. Because love rooted in sacrifice and self-abandonment is not the love I deserve.

When I started giving only clean yeses, everything changed. My relationships got healthier. My resentment lessened. I became more honest about what I truly needed.

It wasn't easy. Sometimes I felt selfish or afraid. But it was necessary. Because the people who love you don't want half of you. They want the whole, honest, present version of you.

This change didn't happen quickly. There's no magical switch that instantly makes you good at setting boundaries or communicating them. It's a practice. One that requires self-reflection, uncomfortable honesty, and sometimes those hard, shaky conversations we all dread.

For many of us, boundaries are most often tested in relationships. Romantic, familial, and friendships. And I get it. I used to believe that giving everything I had was a measure of love or loyalty. I poured myself out for others, convinced that self-sacrifice proved how much I cared.

But love without boundaries is like trying to fill a leaky bucket. You can keep pouring water in, but it will never be enough. The bucket ends up empty. And no one wins.

Setting boundaries taught me that saying "no" doesn't mean I love someone less. Sometimes, "no" is the most loving thing I can say, because it allows me to protect my energy, my heart, and my identity.

Boundaries also clarify relationships.
They create safety.
They build mutual respect.
They say, *"I love you enough to show up for you as my whole self, not a version of me that's drained, resentful, or broken."*

Learning to communicate boundaries wasn't easy for me. Maybe it's not easy for you either. If you're anything like I was, you might be afraid of how people will respond. You might worry about hurting their feelings, losing relationships, or coming across as "difficult."

And honestly? You might unintentionally hurt someone's feelings.
You might lose a relationship.
People might think you're difficult.

You have to learn to be okay with that.

Healthy communication and boundaries go hand in hand. You can't set a boundary without expressing it. And expressing it requires courage. Especially when the conversation feels hard.

I remember one moment when I first communicated a boundary that terrified me. A close and very important friend would constantly unload her problems on me at all hours, pulling me into her chaos like I was a lifeboat she couldn't let go of.

I cared about her deeply. But I started feeling drained, suffocated, and overwhelmed. Every time my phone buzzed, I tensed up, dreading what might come next.

Finally, I sat her down, heart pounding, and said, *"I love you. I want to support you, but I need to protect my own peace, too. I can't always be available to help you fix everything. Can we figure out another way to support each other without it feeling so heavy for me?"*

To my surprise, she understood. Maybe not right away. But the more we talked, the more she grasped what I was saying. More than that, she respected it.

That boundary allowed me to show up for her *and* for myself. Something I couldn't do when I was running on empty.

The hardest conversations often end up being the most healing.

Healthy communication isn't about getting it perfect. It's about being honest, clear, and kind. It's about saying,
*"This is what I need, and I hope we can meet each other there."*

If this feels overwhelming to you, start small.
Boundaries don't have to be big declarations.

Maybe it's saying, *"I can't take that call right now, but I'll check in later."*
Maybe it's telling someone, *"I need some time for myself today."*
Maybe it's choosing not to explain every "no" you give, because you don't have to justify your needs to anyone.

Boundaries will stretch and challenge you.
Some people won't like them.
But the people who respect your boundaries?
They're the ones you want in your life, anyway.
The rest? Let them go.

At the end of the day, setting boundaries and giving only clean yeses is about reclaiming yourself. It's about saying, *"I matter. My needs matter. My voice matters."*

So take a breath and ask yourself:
What's the one boundary I need to set today?
What's one clean yes I want to give?

Start there.

Because when you learn to communicate your needs, honor your "no," and only say "yes" when you truly mean it,
you begin to redefine your life.

You begin to truly live as your whole, empowered, and unapologetic self.

# Chapter Sixteen

# Rebuilding Relationships After Change

*"Letting go means to come to the realization that some people are a part of your history, but not a part of your destiny."*

**Steve Maraboli**

L osing relationships, whether by choice, distance, or circumstance, brought me a different kind of pain. It wasn't just loss; it was a shift in identity, a reordering of my world. I had to learn how to grieve that loss in a healthy way, to process it without letting it harden me. At the same time, I had to take responsibility for the relationships the old me had damaged. Growth brought things to the surface I hadn't expected, and part of becoming the best version of myself meant facing them head-on.

I also had to face something even harder. The truth is that not every fractured relationship was broken *because* I grew. Some were already broken because of who I was before. The version of me that was living in survival mode, reacting from pain, resentment, fear, and exhaustion. I made choices from that place that hurt people. I burned bridges. I shut people out. I lashed out. I showed up in ways that caused damage.

And even though I've grown, though I've done the work, and I continue to do the work, growth doesn't undo the past. Healing doesn't rewrite history. Some relationships were lost not because they couldn't accept the new me, but because the old me caused harm that couldn't be undone.

That's a hard truth to hold. And yet, it's part of the story.

Growth doesn't mean we get to skip accountability. It means we carry the responsibility to acknowledge who we were, what we've done, and what we're choosing to become. Not with shame, but with honesty. With compassion. With ownership.

Some relationships couldn't be rebuilt, not because I didn't want to, but because the damage was already too deep. And I've had to learn to live with that, too. To forgive myself without erasing what happened. To make peace with what I broke, even as I committed to never repeating it.

The people who loved me in my lowest seasons, the ones I lost anyway, deserve to be acknowledged here. Their presence mattered. And their absence still stings.

When I started changing, I expected relief. I thought this newfound clarity, this sense of who I was, this inner strength, would bring me nothing but peace. What I didn't expect was the loneliness that followed. What I didn't anticipate was the tension it created in some of my relationships.

Not everyone was happy about my growth.

That realization hit me hard. Because people matter to me. They always have. Even though I grew up in hardship, I learned to not only crave but cherish human connection. And while I wasn't always successful, my life had been built around other people and around saying yes, showing up, and going the extra mile. We've already unpacked some of that in previous chapters. What I didn't realize was how much my identity was tied to my role in their lives. When I began to change, a void opened up, and I wasn't prepared for it.

Some of my relationships were likely always destined to strain under the weight of my growth. The more I said no, the more I spoke my truth, the more I stopped overextending myself to accommodate others, the more friction I encountered. Some relationships strengthened. Others stayed the same. But the ones that felt strained were the hardest of all. These were the people I had been closest to, and it felt as if my decision to grow had disrupted an unspoken agreement to stay the same.

And sometimes, the smallest things revealed the biggest truths.

I remember one friend in particular. We had always met at a Mexican restaurant in the next town over because she loved it. I tolerated it, but I never really enjoyed it. Occasionally, I'd suggest somewhere else, but she would override me, and so, to that same restaurant, we would go.

One day, I simply said, "I'd love to have lunch with you, but I don't want to eat there again. How about we try something different?"

She got frustrated. She got angry. And in that moment, I realized something. I had never been worth switching restaurants for.

It seems so trivial now, but at the time, it hurt. And it wasn't about the food. It was about the imbalance in our friendship. It showed me something I had ignored for years. Our dynamic only worked as long as I was the one bending. And when I stopped, the cracks became visible.

This happened in more ways than one. I had spent so much of my life saying yes that when I started saying no, people struggled. It felt like telling a petulant child, "No, you can't have this candy," and actually sticking to it despite the tantrum that followed.

But sometimes, the biggest fractures weren't in friendships, they were in the places I once called home.

As I grew into a healthier version of myself, I started to question things within our local church. These weren't small things; they were major issues that impacted our church family and our community. When I spoke up, when I asked the hard questions and tried to address them with both love and honesty, I was shut down.

I went from being welcomed with open arms to being quietly pushed out. Invitations disappeared. Conversations ended when I entered the room. People I had once trusted turned away.

So, yes, I faced resistance. And you might too.

People may misinterpret your growth as rejection. Some may feel threatened by your boundaries because they benefited from the old version of you. This happened with family members who had come to rely on my over giving. The old me showed up. Picked up the pieces. Dropped everything, no matter what, every single time they called. And when I stopped? When I let them figure things out for themselves? They didn't like it.

Others may not understand why you're changing at all.

Imagine a game where the rules have stayed the same for years. Every player knows their role, the rhythm, the expectations. And then, suddenly, you change the rules. But you don't tell the other players. They struggle. They get frustrated. They don't understand why things feel different. That's what happens when you begin to grow and not everyone will be ready to celebrate your transformation.

And that's okay.

The people meant to walk with you will adjust. The ones who won't, well, that's their choice.

## Communicating Your Growth.

As I grew, I began to realize that change alone wasn't enough. I also had to *communicate* that change. I had spent too many years stuffing things down, avoiding conflict, and going along just to keep the peace. I didn't know how to let people into the shifts happening inside me because, truthfully; I was still learning how to understand them myself.

It wasn't easy at first. When you've spent a lifetime shaping yourself to meet everyone else's expectations, finding the words to speak your truth can feel terrifying. I worried about how people would respond. Would they be angry? Confused? Would they think I was being selfish or dramatic? Would they leave?

But over time, I learned that staying silent was its own kind of betrayal. One I wasn't willing to keep repeating. So I started trying. I began to express my needs more clearly. Not with blame, but with honesty. Not with anger, but with love.

I reminded myself that no one else lives inside my mind. They don't feel the tension I carry, or see the growth happening in the quiet moments. If I wanted people to understand the woman I was becoming, I had to give them something to hold on to. Words, clarity, truth.

Some of those conversations were gentle. Others were hard. Sometimes I stumbled through them, heart pounding, voice shaking. But I kept going. Because clarity is a kindness, not just to others, but to myself.

There were people who didn't understand. I remember someone once saying, "You must think you're better than us now." It stung. Because that wasn't the truth at all. I didn't think I was better. I just knew I wanted to be *different*. And I had fought hard for that difference.

Still, not everyone walked away. Some people I thought would drift... stayed. They saw me. They met me where I was. They didn't need me to be who I was before in order to love me now.

That meant everything.

Growth taught me that not all relationships are meant to evolve, but the ones that are, will. The people who are meant to stay won't require me to shrink. They won't punish me for growing. They'll adjust. Just like I had to.

And the people who can't? That's not mine to carry.

## Letting Go With Love

Growth sometimes requires letting go.

Not every relationship is meant to last forever. Some were only ever meant for a season. Others were tolerated because we weren't yet whole enough to see the truth.

You don't owe anyone a version of yourself that you've outgrown.

And it's okay to grieve those losses. It's okay to mourn relationships that fade. It doesn't mean you're making the wrong choice; it means you're choosing yourself.

Walking away doesn't mean you don't care. It just means you care about yourself, too. And sometimes, it doesn't mean goodbye forever. Some relationships don't have to end completely. They just need time. A pause. A space to breathe.

I recognize that the old me, as it was transforming into the new me, caused some damage. And I carry hope that, in time, some of those relationships can be repaired. Growth doesn't erase the past, but it does offer the possibility of something new. Some connections might find their way back in a healthier, more aligned way. Others may remain part of my history, and that's okay too.

There are also some relationships I've chosen not to rebuild, and one of those was with my father.

I won't go into every detail here, but the damage in that relationship ran deep. And for a long time, I held onto the hope that one day, things would be different. That one day, I'd say the right thing, or he would change, or we'd somehow find common ground.

But as I grew, I began to see the toll that relationship had taken on me. The pain it kept reopening. The ways it distorted how I saw myself. There came a point where I had to stop trying to resurrect something that was never whole to begin with. I had to accept that not all bridges were meant to be rebuilt.

Forgiveness doesn't always mean reconciliation. Sometimes, it means letting go with peace in your heart and boundaries that protect your healing.

The important thing is knowing that healing isn't always the same. Some relationships will return stronger. Others may stay at a distance. And some were never meant to be reclaimed. But no matter the outcome, I've learned that honoring my growth means allowing things to unfold as they're meant to, without forcing, without guilt, and without abandoning myself in the process.

The relationships that truly matter will adjust.

The ones that don't? Let them go. With love. And without guilt.

You are not responsible for making other people comfortable with your growth.

You are responsible for honoring the person you are becoming.

# Chapter Seventeen

---

# Keep Going, You're Becoming

*"Courage doesn't always roar. Sometimes courage is the quiet voice at the end of the day saying, 'I will try again tomorrow.'"*
— **Mary Anne Radmacher**

I wish I could tell you that everything fell into place the moment I decided to disrupt my default. That once I learned about boundaries, communication, self-love, and joy, I stopped stumbling altogether. That every step forward felt steady, and every choice was crystal clear.

The truth?

Change is hard. Growth is uncomfortable. And the path forward has been anything but smooth or predictable.

Learning to live differently hasn't meant I always get it right. I've made mistakes. More than I can count. In my eagerness to grow, I sometimes swung too far in the other direction. I spoke too sharply when I finally found my voice. I avoided conflict when I should have stayed present. I judged others, sometimes harshly, maybe because I was still afraid of being judged myself. And too often, I let fear take the wheel, whispering cruel lies I'd worked so hard to unlearn.

You'll lose the people you love.
They don't really love you.
The bottom is going to fall out any moment now.

There were also moments I simply ran out of steam. Despite everything I had learned, despite all the work I had done, I still lost motivation. I felt tired. Worn thin. I questioned whether it was even worth it. Would I ever actually see the life I was working toward, or was I chasing a vision that would never fully arrive?

But those moments, the ones where everything feels heavy and hope feels like a stranger, aren't failures. They're invitations. Quiet checkpoints. Gentle reminders to pause, breathe, and ask myself a question I now return to often.

**Why did I start?**

When I couldn't rely on others to keep me moving, I had to learn how to be my own encourager. I had to build an inner voice strong enough to counter the fear and doubt. At first, that voice was small, more whisper than roar, but it was there. And the more I chose to listen, the steadier it became. Until eventually, it was a voice I could trust.

I kept going because I believed in the life I was creating and the woman I was becoming. I knew she was worth fighting for.

There were lessons I carried with me like a roadmap:
That boundaries aren't walls, they're bridges back to peace.
That honest communication, even when it's hard, is what makes real connection possible.
That self-love is a necessity, not a luxury.
That joy is something we choose, not something we wait for.
That my beliefs can evolve. That my strength can multiply.
And that my life, messy, imperfect, unfinished, is worth showing up for.

There were still days when I questioned everything. When I packed up my life and moved across the country, there were nights I sat on the floor of my new kitchen, surrounded by a pile of unopened boxes and essentials, and wondered if I'd made a mistake. I had left so much behind. People, places, pieces of who I had been. I felt brave and terrified all at once.

And then one day, in the middle of that transition, I found something I thought I had lost.

A small binder ring filled with index cards. Each one holding a quote, a scripture, or a piece of encouragement I had collected during my disruption journey. Pages and pages of the very words that had gotten me through.

I sat there on the floor, tears rolling down my cheeks, holding those cards like they were sacred. Because they were. They had carried me. They had reminded me of who I was becoming. And at that moment, they reminded me again.

It was never about arriving at some perfect destination.
It was about continuing.

Trying again.

Listening to the quiet voice inside me that says, *"I will try again tomorrow."*

I've learned that growth isn't about perfection. It's about courage. It's about persistence. It's about making the choice, again and again, to keep becoming, even when it's hard. Especially when it's hard.

I used to live from fear. From people-pleasing. From patterns I didn't even realize I was repeating. I held on tightly to people, to expectations, to versions of myself that no longer served me, because I thought if I let go, everything would fall apart.

But letting go didn't break me.

It made room for peace.

It made room for me.

And yes, there are still moments when the old fear creeps in. When I feel like maybe, I'm not doing enough or being enough or getting it right. But I've learned to pause. To breathe. To listen for the steady voice that lives within me now.

She doesn't shout.

She doesn't demand.

She simply says, keep going.

Every time I choose myself, my boundaries, my healing, my truth, my joy, I take one more step toward the life I'm building.

So if you're tired, if you've stumbled, if you've doubted yourself more times than you can count, let me say this clearly;

You're still becoming.

And becoming is brave.
It's beautiful.
And it's enough.

Keep going.

# Chapter Eighteen

---

# Keep Creating

*"And suddenly you just know... it's time to start something new and trust the magic of beginnings."*
**—Meister Eckhart**

There's something disorienting about what comes after healing. After the disruption. After the transformation. After the clarity.

You'd think it would feel peaceful. Settled. Resolved. And sometimes, it does.

But more often, it feels quiet. Almost too quiet.

Because once the dust settles, there's no chaos to fight.

No fire to put out.

No old version of you to shed.

There's just you.

Standing at the edge of what comes next. Wondering where to place your foot.

That's the line between who you were and who you're willing to become.

I didn't always understand that. I used to believe that once I healed, once I set the boundaries, found my voice, and let go of what no longer served me, life would split wide open in some dramatic, dazzling way.

And in some ways, it did.

But in other ways, it got quieter. Slower. More deliberate.
Less like a breakthrough and more like a blank canvas.

Healing gives you clarity,
but creating what comes next?

That demands something deeper.
It demands courage.
The kind that doesn't wait for applause.
The kind that stands at the edge of everything you've known and whispers, *Now what?*

It asks, *Are you willing to become someone new, without proof it will work out?*
*Are you willing to live out the wisdom you fought so hard to earn?*
*Are you willing to rise not just from what broke you, but toward what builds you?*

That's the kind of courage I didn't know I had.

Until one day, I was invited to speak to a group of women at a business retreat.

The invitation caught me off guard. I wasn't a polished speaker. I wasn't sure if I belonged in that room.

My hands shook. My voice trembled. And I kept asking myself, *Who am I to teach anyone else these lessons? I'm still living* with them.

But I showed up anyway.

The thing about teaching; real, from-the-heart, truth-telling teaching, is that it's not just for your audience. It's for you, too. When you speak something aloud, it takes root in a new way. It asks you to believe it. To own it. And when you forget the stage voice, when you speak from the gut, not the script, something honest breaks through. That's what happened that day.

As I shared pieces of my story; disrupting my patterns, reclaiming my worth, and building a life I didn't have to run from, everything in the room got a little quieter.

The energy changed.
It got braver. Heavier. More alive.

Heads nodded. Eyes welled up.
Walls dropped.

And one by one, women started opening up about their fears, their false starts, the parts of themselves they were still trying to piece together.

That's when it hit me:

I didn't need to be perfect to be powerful.
I didn't need to have all the answers to make an impact.
I just had to tell the truth. Unfiltered, unpolished, and all mine.

Then came a question that stopped me in my tracks.

Midway through the conversation, a woman raised her hand and asked,

**"What about creating what's next? Like actually creating it. Is that part of** this, **too?"**

I paused.

My mind scrambled for the kind of answer I thought I was supposed to give.
Manifesting. Vision boards. Alignment. Buzzwords I'd seen all over my feed.
It all sounded shiny and packaged, and just a little too perfect.

But none of that alone was how I got here.
That wasn't my path. Not exactly.

But her question lingered.

And later, I realized I had been creating my future all along. Just not in the way most people talked about it.

Not through wishful thinking or perfect routines.
Not through magical timing or miracle formulas.
But through quiet, intentional choices full of faith and belief.

Through setting boundaries, even when it was hard.
Through choosing joy, even when it felt distant.
Through walking away from people and patterns I once clung to.
Through telling myself, again and again, *You are allowed to build something different.*

That's how I began to shape what came next. Not by waiting for the stars to align, but by aligning with who I wanted to become.

And let me tell you, it wasn't glamorous.

It looked like shaky starts and awkward conversations.
Like crying in the kitchen because I missed the familiar.
Like rereading quotes on index cards just to remember what I believed.
Like showing up to a new life in a new place, unsure of where to begin.

But I kept going. Because I believed, deep down, that the life I was building was worth the discomfort of becoming someone new. And, I could see it! It was there. It was created, and it was being created.

Creating is about the small, sacred work of becoming.
The kind that doesn't make headlines, but reshapes your life anyway.

It's about knowing that vision boards and big dreams mean nothing without integrity, aligned action, and a willingness to stay with yourself when the road gets quiet.

You don't create what's next by snapping your fingers.
You create it by showing up.
You create it by asking yourself;
*What do I truly want?*
*What am I willing to release to make space for it?*
*What kind of person do I want to be while I build it?*

And then you move.
Even when the fear creeps in.
Even when the old version of you begs for comfort.
Even when the people around you don't understand.

You move anyway.

Becoming who you're meant to be will always feel like a risk. But it's one worth taking.

You don't need to get it all right. You just need to keep choosing what feels aligned.
You don't need a master plan. You just need to trust the next step.
You don't need to rush. You just need to begin.

Again and again and again.

And when the doubts whisper, when they tell you it's too late, or you're too tired, or this is too big, pause. Breathe. Remember who you've become. And remember why you started.

Seeing what comes next isn't found by looking backward.
It's created by what you choose right now.

And you, my friend, are more ready than you think.

# Part 4

---

Conclusion

Shadow Scribe Media

# Chapter Nineteen

---

# You Hold The Pen

*"I am not what happened to me, I am what I choose to become."*
— **Carl Jung**

As we reach the final pages of *Disrupt Your Default*, I want to invite you to pause. To breathe. To take in just how far we've come.

You've walked with me through stories of hardship, healing, clarity, and courage, and I don't take that lightly. Writing this book meant opening some of the most vulnerable corners of my life and laying them bare on the page. But somewhere along the way, this stopped being just my story.

It became ours.
And now, it's yours too.

This book began as an offering. A gentle but firm reminder that life does not have to stay the way it's always been. That you are not bound to your pain, your past, or the patterns that once shaped you. That you can disrupt what no longer serves you, and build something better.

It's a bold promise.
But it's also a true one.

## Looking Back at How Far We've Come

When you first picked up this book, maybe you were tired, bone-deep tired of the cycle you couldn't seem to break. Maybe you didn't even know what needed to change. You just knew something had to.

And still, you showed up.
That matters.

Showing up is always the first courageous step.
It's what cracks the door open to everything that comes next.

We started by looking back. At the old wounds. At the patterns. At the silent agreements you made to survive a life that wasn't built for your becoming the best version of yourself. That work is not easy. It takes grit and grace to turn toward your truth instead of away from it.

But that's where healing begins.
And healing is what sets you free.

From there, we moved through growth, not the kind that explodes overnight, but the kind that roots quietly and holds steady. We talked about boundaries, not as barricades, but as lifelines. We explored self-love, not the fluffy kind, but the fierce kind. The kind that says, *Even if no one else shows up for me, I will.*

We reclaimed joy, not as something you earn, but something you choose.
We challenged the mindsets that kept you small.

We named the dreams you buried.
We started to believe you were worth the life you imagined.

Each chapter has been a step. Not toward perfection, but toward alignment. Toward intention. Toward wholeness.

And now, here you are. At the close of this book. But not at the end of your journey.

Because there is no final arrival.
No mountaintop where everything becomes easy.
Just the daily work of becoming.

And that's where your power lives. In the choosing.
Over and over again.

## A Gentle Reminder: Progress Over Perfection

Let me leave you with this. You're not meant to get it all right.

Growth is not a straight line. Healing is not a checklist. You will fall back into old patterns. You will have days when it all feels too heavy. You will question yourself, your strength, and whether you're capable of continuing.

When that happens, pause.
Come back to this truth...

Every time you chose to believe in yourself, even when it felt impossible, it mattered.
Every time you responded differently, even when it took everything in you, it mattered.

Every truth you spoke, every boundary you honored, every moment of self-kindness, it all counts.

I often think of the potter shaping clay. Her hands press and pull, forming something new from what once felt shapeless. Sometimes the clay collapses. Sometimes it cracks. But she doesn't toss it aside.

She begins again.

Because she knows the beauty is in the process.

And so it is with you.

You are the artist.
This is your life.
And every imperfect, bold, beautiful step forward is shaping something extraordinary.

## A Call to Keep Going

What you've done here, the rethinking, the reclaiming, the redefining, it doesn't end when you close this book.

It begins again. Right now.

You can return to what's familiar. Or you can take what you've learned and choose differently. You can honor your healing. You can love yourself without condition. You can rise. Again and again. Even when it's hard.

You can choose you.
You can choose growth.
You can choose to stay awake to the life that's calling you.

And when you fall (because we all do), you get back up. Not because it's easy. But because *you're worth it.*

Your dreams are worth it.
The life you're building is worth it.

## Paint the Picture of Your Future

So, what now?

Close your eyes and see her. The version of you who disrupted her default. Who dropped the old stories and wrote new ones. Who walks through the world with clarity, courage, and grace.

What does her life feel like?
How does she carry herself?
What has she released? What has she claimed?

I see her.
She's not a fantasy.
She's not a someday version.

She's already in you.
Every step you take brings you closer to her.

## Closing Thoughts: A Promise to Yourself

Before we part ways, let me remind you of a few truths.

You are not your past.
You are not your pain.
You are not the limits others placed on you.

You are powerful.
You are resilient.
You are worthy of a life that feels whole and honest and true.

This book was never about giving you all the answers.
It was about handing you back the pen.

To remind you that you get to write the next chapter.
On your terms.
In your time.
With your voice.

So take a deep breath.
Take one step forward.
And keep going.

Because the life you want?

It's closer than you think.
It's waiting for you to claim it.
And you, my friend, are ready.

Thank you for walking this path with me.

And if you stumble, know this,
You're not starting over.
You're starting again.

This time, with more truth.
More courage.
More love.

**You hold the pen now. Write something beautiful.**

# Chapter Twenty

---

# The Disruptor's Toolkit

## A Note Before You Begin the Toolkit

I didn't have many friends growing up.

You already know my early years were difficult, marked by experiences no child should ever have to carry. Loneliness became a quiet companion in those days. It settled in early and made itself at home.

With no steady presence to guide me, no close friendships or role models to light the way, I turned to the only refuge I could find: books and journals.

Books became my sanctuary. Between the pages, I found safety, adventure, and characters who faced unimaginable struggles and still found a way through. I clung to their courage, their resilience, their ability to rise. Each story whispered something different. They gave me hope, wisdom, or simply the reminder that I wasn't alone.

And then there were my journals.

If books were where I escaped, journaling was how I came home. On those pages, I could be completely honest without judgment, without shame. I poured out fears, dreams, frustrations, and questions I didn't dare ask out loud. My journals became old friends, always waiting for me to return. They held my tears, my joy, my wondering. They were my safe space before I ever knew what that meant.

Over time, those books and journals became more than just paper and ink. They became my mentors.
When I didn't know how to dream, they taught me.
When I couldn't find my voice, they gave me language.
When the world felt too dark, they reminded me there was still light. If I was willing to look for it.

As I grew and stumbled and grew again, I realized that life is a journey, and every journey needs tools. Not the kind you carry only in your hands, but the kind you also carry in your heart. Truths. Reminders. Practices. Small lifelines that keep you steady when everything feels shaky.

So I built myself a toolbox.

Not a just physical one, but a sacred space where I could return to the lessons I'd gathered. A quiet place to remember what I knew deep down. Over time, that toolbox became an anchor. A compass. And sometimes, a gentle nudge to keep going when I wasn't sure I could.

In this book, I've shared parts of that journey. The pain that shaped me. The lessons that saved me. The moments that called me back to life. And while I can't hand you everything I've collected, I want to offer you a few of the tools that continue to serve me. Ones I hope will meet you where you are and walk with you as you keep moving forward.

You don't need all the answers today. You don't need to have it all figured out.
Life isn't about certainty. It's about courage. The courage to show up. To try again. To believe there's something better waiting, even when you can't see it yet.

So let this be your reminder. You are not alone. You carry more wisdom and strength than you know. And on the days when you forget, when doubt creeps in or you need something solid to hold onto, come back here. To these words. These tools. This truth.

Your life is yours to shape. Your story is still being written.
No matter where you begin, no matter how many times you fall, you always have the power to pick up the pen and begin again.

This is my offering to you. Pieces of my toolbox passed from my heart to yours.
May they serve you well.

## Disruptor Journal Prompts

### Part One: Rethink – Reflecting on the Past + Reclaiming Your Voice

- What is one belief you've carried since childhood that no longer fits who you are?

- Write about a moment in your life that shaped how you see yourself. What did you internalize? What are you ready to release?

- When did you first feel invisible or unheard? How did that moment shape your voice?

- What survival strategies helped you cope in hard seasons, and which ones are you ready to outgrow?

- Who influenced your sense of worth growing up (for better or worse)? How do you reclaim that worth now?

- What is one truth you've buried under fear, people-pleasing, or perfectionism? What would happen if you gave it space?

- What story from your past are you ready to stop telling yourself?

- If your younger self met you today, what would surprise or inspire them?

- What have you overcome that you don't give yourself enough credit for?

- How has looking back with honesty helped you move forward with more power?

## Part Two: Reclaim – Returning to Wholeness + Rewriting Beliefs

- What does self-love *feel* like, not just look like, for you?

- List five things you deeply appreciate about yourself, even if they're messy or imperfect.

- When was the last time you said yes when your body, heart, or gut said no? What stopped you from honoring yourself?

- What boundary have you set that changed your life for the better?

- Where are your boundaries weakest, and what's the cost of keeping them blurry?

- Write a letter of forgiveness to your past self for the ways you abandoned your needs.

- How can you practice more self-compassion in moments you feel inadequate?

- What negative self-talk still plays on a loop in your mind, and how can you reframe it with truth?

- Who would you become if you no longer questioned your worth?

- What belief have you recently rewritten that created a noticeable shift in how you live?

## Part Three: Redefine – Choosing Again + Creating a New Way Forward

- What's a dream you've quietly held that you're now ready to speak aloud?

- Imagine your future self living fully and freely. What does she believe? What does she no longer tolerate?

- What's one small action you can take today that aligns with the life you want to create?

- What does growth mean to you now, after everything you've survived?

- Write about a mistake that taught you something essential about yourself.

- What does joy look like in your everyday life? How can you make space for more of it?

- How can you celebrate progress instead of waiting for perfection?

- What are you currently afraid to try, and what would become possible if you did it anyway?

- What new default are you intentionally creating?

- What will you no longer apologize for as you move boldly toward your future?

## Disruptor Affirmations

*Speak them. Write them. Believe them. Let them become part of you.*

These affirmations aren't just pretty words.

They're reminders. Replacements.

A way to rewrite the internal script that's been running on autopilot for too long. Use them daily, or when you need to remember who you are and what you're capable of.

## Affirmations for Growth & Change

- I am no longer bound by who I was. I choose who I become.

- Every small shift I make creates momentum.

- I welcome change, even when it feels uncomfortable.

- I release the need to stay the same in order to be accepted.

- I trust the process of becoming, even when I can't see what's next.

## Affirmations for Self-Love & Worthiness

- I am worthy of love, rest, and joy without conditions.

- My imperfections are not flaws. They are reminders that I am real.

- I choose to be kind to myself, even when I am growing.

- I no longer wait to be "enough." I already am.

- I deserve to take up space in my own life.

## Affirmations for Strength & Resilience

- I have survived every hard thing I once thought would break me.

- I am resilient, not because I never fall, but because I always rise.

- My past has shaped me, but it does not define me.

- I can be soft and strong, broken and brave, all at once.

- I hold power in my ability to begin again.

## Affirmations for Boundaries & Belonging

- My boundaries are not walls. They are bridges to deeper connection.

- Saying "no" is not rejection. It's self-respect.

- I do not owe anyone access to me at the expense of my peace.

- I can be loving and firm at the same time.

- I belong everywhere. I decide to show up as my full self.

## Affirmations for Joy & Gratitude

- I notice the beauty in small things and let them move me.

- Joy is not a reward, it's a practice I choose daily.

- I don't need perfect circumstances to feel grateful.

- I allow laughter, lightness, and delight to exist alongside the hard.

- I celebrate my life with all its ordinary magic.

## Affirmations for Presence & Peace

- I am here. I am grounded. I am safe at this moment.

- I release the past and trust what is unfolding.

- I choose calm over chaos, even when the world feels loud.

- I don't need to rush. I trust the pace of my journey.

- In stillness, I return to myself.

## Affirmations for Redefining & Manifesting

- I give myself full permission to dream differently.

- I align my thoughts, beliefs, and actions with what I truly desire.

- I am allowed to change directionand change my mind.

- I no longer shrink to fit spaces I've outgrown.

- I trust that what is meant for me will meet me when I'm ready, and I'm getting ready now.

## Book Club Reflections

*Conversation starters for the disruptors, the seekers, and the bold-hearted.*

Use these questions to reflect deeply, speak honestly, and explore what this book stirred up in you.

Let the conversation go beyond the page and into your story.

## Big Picture Reflections

- Which chapter or section has impacted you most, and why?

- What part of Mea's story felt the most relatable to your own?

- How has your understanding of "default mode" shifted after reading this book?

- If you had to summarize the book's core message in one sentence, what would it be?

- What are you walking away with that you didn't expect?

## On Beliefs & Inner Voice

- What's one belief you recognized in yourself that you're ready to disrupt?

- Did any part of this book help you better understand where that belief came from?

- What does your inner voice sound like now, and how do you want it to sound moving forward?

## On Self-Love, Boundaries & Reclaiming Your Power

- How has your relationship with self-love evolved over the years, and did this book shift it further?

- What boundary are you currently setting, or struggling to set?

- Where have you been abandoning yourself in small, unnoticed ways? How will you return?

## On Growth, Gratitude & Joy

- When was the last time you experienced joy in something simple? Did this book help you notice that more?

- How do you define growth now, and how do you track it without relying on outside validation?

- What's one habit, thought, or belief that you're choosing to release?

## On Redefining & Moving Forward

- What does it mean to you to redefine your life on your own terms?

- What dream or desire are you finally ready to stop hiding from?

- What's one new belief or practice you're walking away with after finishing this book?

- If your "next chapter" had a title, what would it be?

## Group Practice Prompts

Use these for deeper discussion, journaling together, or as creative challenges:

- Write a letter to your past self, and share a sentence or phrase from it aloud.

- Each person names one belief they're disrupting, and the action they'll take this week.

- Do a "clean yes / clean no" check-in: What are you currently saying yes to that isn't aligned?

- Share one affirmation from the book that you're claiming for yourself, and why.

- Create a group accountability challenge: Each person chooses one small daily shift to commit to for the next 7 days.

## Recommended Reading

*A curated list to support your journey of rethinking, reclaiming, and redefining your life.*
These books have been selected to align with the heart of *Disrupt Your Default.* Each one offering wisdom, tools, or perspective to support the bold changes you're making.

You don't need to read them all. Choose what speaks to your season and let the rest wait until you're ready.

### To Help You Rethink the Past & Rewrite Your Beliefs

- *The Mountain Is You* by Brianna Wiest

- *Mindset: The New Psychology of Success* by Carol S. Dweck

- *The Four Agreements* by Don Miguel Ruiz

- *Man's Search for Meaning* by Viktor E. Frankl

- *The Gifts of Imperfection* by Brené Brown

### To Help You Reclaim Your Voice, Boundaries, and Self-Worth

- *Set Boundaries, Find Peace* by Nedra Glover Tawwab

- *Untamed* by Glennon Doyle

- *Radical Acceptance* by Tara Brach

- *The Self-Love Experiment* by Shannon Kaiser

- *Daring Greatly* by Brené Brown

### To Help You Redefine Your Life, Dreams, and Possibilities

- *Atomic Habits* by James Clear

- *Everything Is Figureoutable* by Marie Forleo

- *The Universe Has Your Back* by Gabby Bernstein

- *Big Magic* by Elizabeth Gilbert

- *The Alchemist* by Paulo Coelho

## For Healing, Resilience, and Inner Strength

- *What Happened to You?* by Dr. Bruce Perry & Oprah Winfrey

- *The Body Keeps the Score* by Bessel van der Kolk

- *Rising Strong* by Brené Brown

- *Option B* by Sheryl Sandberg & Adam Grant

- *Healing Is Required* by Anika Applewhite

## For Joy, Gratitude & Mindful Living

- *The Book of Joy* by Dalai Lama, Desmond Tutu & Douglas Abrams

- *One Thousand Gifts* by Ann Voskamp

- *Stillness Is the Key* by Ryan Holiday

- *The Power of Now* by Eckhart Tolle

- *Wherever You Go, There You Are* by Jon Kabat-Zinn

**Words That Wake You Up**

**Rethink: Awareness, Courage, and Letting Go**

**Reclaim: Self-Worth, Boundaries, and Bold Love**

**Redefine: Growth, Possibility, and Becoming**

# Chapter
# Twenty-One

---

# It's Just Getting
# Good

Y ou picked up this book searching for something.

    Clarity. Courage.

Proof that change was possible.

And now, here you are, on the other side of these pages, holding something even more powerful than answers.

You hold the ability to choose.

So the question becomes:

**What will you do with it?**

You can set this book down and slip back into what's familiar.

The patterns.

The doubts.
The habits that have kept you where you are.

Or you can do the harder, braver thing.

You can decide, *right now,* that your life is worth disrupting.
You can decide that your past doesn't get the final word.
That fear no longer gets to write your story.
That hesitation no longer gets to run the show.

You can choose the version of you who's waiting on the other side of this work.
The one who speaks with clarity.
Moves with confidence.
Chooses joy.
Embraces possibility.
Lives fully.

And you can choose her. Not someday, not when it's easy, not when everything makes sense.
**Right now. As you are.**

Imperfect. Becoming.
Worthy.

So take a breath.
Take that first step.
And then, take the next one.

Your story isn't over.

**It's just getting good.**
**Now go disrupt everything they said you couldn't become.**

## A Note of Gratitude

Thank you for reading *Disrupt Your Default*.

Writing this book has been one of the most personal, soul-stretching things I've ever done, and I'm honored to have shared it with you.

This is just the beginning. The first in a series of books I'll be releasing in 2025, each one created to help you break free from the habits, beliefs, and limits that no longer serve you, and step into the life that does.

If you'd like a sample chapter of the next book in the series, *Disrupt Your Limits: Bold Moves, Brave Leadership, and Building a Business on Your Terms*, and want to stay updated on release dates, I'd love to connect.

Join my mailing list at meabrown.com

Your journey is yours to create.
And I can't wait to see where it takes you next.

With gratitude,
**Mea Brown**

www.ingramcontent.com/pod-product-compliance
Lightning Source LLC
Chambersburg PA
CBHW060153130626
46556CB00006B/2617